Jaso

Congrats on
the Goodreads comp.

— Clay

FUND
IDE
LIFES

**BUY TIME, FIND NEW EXPERIENCES
AND KEEP MORE OF WHAT YOU'VE WORKED FOR.**

YOUR AL TYLE

CLAYTON DANIEL

FUND YOUR IDEAL LIFESTYLE

**BUY TIME, FIND NEW EXPERIENCES
AND KEEP MORE OF WHAT YOU'VE WORKED FOR.**

CLAYTON DANIEL

First published in Australia in 2017 by XY Publishing
© Clayton Daniel 2017

Clayton Daniel has asserted his right to be identified as the author of this work in accordance with the Australian Copyright Act 1968.

NATIONAL LIBRARY OF AUSTRALIA CATALOGUING-IN-PUBLICATION ENTRY

Author:	Daniel, Clayton, 1983 –
Title:	*Fund Your Ideal Lifestyle: Buy time, find new experiences, and keep more of what you worked for*
ISBN:	978-0-9945780-0-6
Subjects:	Self Actualisation (Motivation) Financial Advice (Finance)
Ordering Information:	Special discounts are available on quantity purchases made by corporations, associations, and others. For details, contact the publisher at www.xyadviser.com
Author Photo:	Jason Malouin
Cover/Interior Design:	Erin Tyler

First Edition
14 13 12 11 10 / 10 9 8 7 6 5 4 3 2 1
www.fundyourideallifestyle.com.au

DISCLAIMER.

This book is designed to provide information the author believes to be accurate on the subject matters covered, but it is sold with the understanding neither the author nor the publisher is offering individual advice tailored to any specific port-folio or to any individual's particular needs, or rendering investment advice or other professional services such as legal, angel investing or accounting advice. A competent professional's service should be sought if one needs expert assistance in areas that include investment, startup, legal, financial advice and accounting.

This book references performance data collected over many time periods and past results do not guarantee future performance. Additionally, performance data, in addition to laws and regulations, change over time, which could change the status of the information in this book. This book solely provides historical data to discuss and illustrate the underlying principles.

Additionally, this book is not intended to serve as the basis for any financial de-cision, recommendations of any specific products, or as an offer to sell or pur-chase any specific investments. Only a prospectus may be used to offer to sell or purchase any financial product or security, and a prospectus must be read and considered carefully before investing or spending money.

No warranty is made with respect to the accuracy or completeness of the informa-tion contained herein, and both the author and the publisher specifically disclaim any responsibility for any liability, loss, or risk, personal or otherwise, which is incurred as a consequence, directly or indirectly, of the use and application of any of the contents of this book. Except insofar as any liability under statute cannot be excluded, the author and publisher do not accept any liability for any error or omission in this book or for any resulting loss or damage suffered by the recipient or any other person.

In the text that follows, people's names and identifying characteristics have been changed to preserve privacy. Clayton Daniel has worked as a tax accountant and as a financial adviser licensed through Hillross Financial Services, and all advice in this book is general in nature and does not constitute as personal financial ad-vice as it does not take in to account your personal objectives, financial situation and needs. Before acting on anything in this book, consider how appropriate it is to your own objectives, needs and financial situation.

TO:

ANYONE WHO STAYED UP ALL NIGHT
TRYING TO FIGURE IT ALL OUT.

I'M WITH YOU.

CONTENTS

PROLOGUE

STEP 1 / CLARIFY LIFESTYLE

STEP 2 / AUTOMATE CASHFLOW

STEP 3 / PURCHASE CAPITAL ASSETS

EPILOGUE

"THE UNEXAMINED LIFE IS NOT WORTH LIVING."

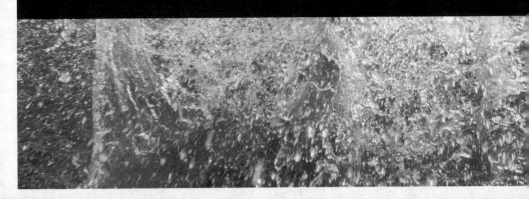

– SOCRATES / *PLATO'S APOLOGY*

AUTHOR'S NOTE

On one hand, writing this book has been one of the hardest things I've ever done. Sitting here in my new apartment, with a view overlooking Sydney is a constant reminder of all the days I missed out on while dumping everything I've ever learned straight into the pages of this book. I don't even want to think about the irony of calling it 'Fund Your Ideal Lifestyle', when I've watched so many beautiful days pass by from my perch in front of a laptop, churning out page after page, only to scrap it all and start again.

On the other hand, it's been a real joy. I love figuring out how to make complex issues sound simple, and I've been doing it for so long in my job that those one-on-one lessons translated to the page quite smoothly. It's also given me a chance to exercise some pent-up prose I've collected over the years through my penchant for the 'word of the day'.[1]

However, the book is now complete, and hopefully, it does as it's intended: provide a 'how to' guide on deciding what you want out of life, and creating an implementable process for you to achieve it. No small feat I know, and the weight of that mandate isn't lost on me; I promise you that.

---

1 / Except I didn't find a way to use the word 'circumlocution' anywhere. It's succinct language to describe the act of not using succinct language to describe. Phenomenal

But before we get started, let's first set the parameters. I didn't write this book to make you rich. There are enough of those out there already. And I didn't write this book to show you how to 'escape the rat race'. Again, the bookstore aisles are full of them.

Instead, I wrote this book to help you create a life you're happy to live day in day out, without the need to 'escape' – a life you enjoy from the time you wake up, 'til the time your head hits the pillow again.

The motivation for this book came from the endless hours I spent talking to clients about their money and in turn their lives. I realised the proverbial carrot we are meant to all chase – sitting on the beach not doing anything – was in reality, rarely what people described as I teased out their plans and hopes for the future.

Despite what we've all been told to strive for, the age-old fantasy of building a fortune, and retiring young on passive income to lounge in a hammock as the sun sets over azure water, wasn't the existential pinnacle for which most people were aiming.

Instead, it was building a fulfilling life through hitting career milestones, being able to spend more time with friends and family, getting away every now and again, and being able to put money aside for later in life.

It wasn't glossy magazine covers; it was real life done well. And after listening to their plans and seeing how their money management affected the outcome, I realised my clients' passions and desires were similar to mine. They wanted to know they were making the most out of their time and resources. All they needed was someone with a bit more experience in these fields to help them do it. It was as simple as that (and as difficult).

And if it weren't for the personal and professional experiences that shaped my life, I would never have assumed I could write this book. But assuming we aren't living in the Infinite Monkey Theorem[2], here we are.

So before we get started, know this book comes from both my head and my heart. You're probably closer to living your ideal lifestyle than you think; this book is just here to get you over the line.

Cheers,

CLAYTON

---

2 / A bizarre theory which states given an infinite amount of monkeys hitting keys on type writers for an infinite amount of time, they will almost surely produce every literary work ever created.

PR
LO

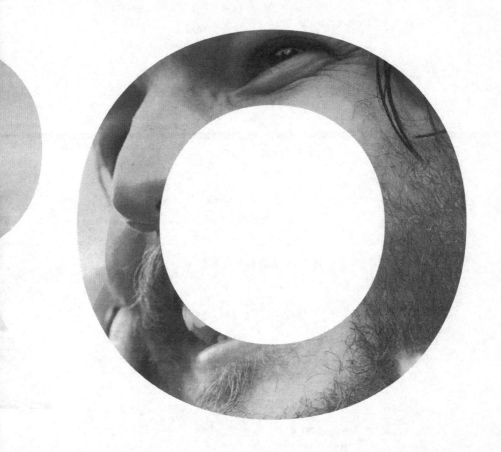

AN AMATEUR ROCKSTAR FROM THE END OF THE WORLD

"YOU HAVE BRAINS IN YOUR HEAD.

YOU HAVE FEET IN YOUR SHOES.

YOU CAN STEER YOURSELF

ANY DIRECTION YOU CHOOSE.

YOU'RE ON YOUR OWN.

AND YOU KNOW WHAT YOU KNOW.

AND YOU ARE THE GUY

WHO'LL DECIDE WHERE TO GO."

– DR. SEUSS / *OH THE PLACE YOU'LL GO!*

"I LIKE IT WHEN A FLOWER OR A LITTLE TUFT OF GRASS

GROWS THROUGH A CRACK IN THE CONCRETE.

IT'S SO F****N' HEROIC."

– GEORGE CARLIN

W e huddle together and throw our arms around each other, not just to protect our space and keep the outside world away, but so we can hear one another speak. There's a lot of noise going on, a crowd of teenagers can be rather rowdy like that.

Surrounding us are people holding cameras, people talking into headsets, and people writing on notepads, but that's none of our business at the moment. We have five more minutes to wade in the outrageous reality we have created for ourselves over the last six years and want to savour it for one last moment before we join the real world again.

And as we stand there, sweat falling over each other; we know we have just one thing left to do. We wait to see if the undulating sea of flesh starts screaming for an encore.

It's at this moment you're at the mercy of the crowd. The fate of the night hangs on their collective reaction. If they scream for one last song, you're a rock god. If they don't, you go home a nobody.

And tonight is, in fact, a very big night. It's the launch of our debut EP, and confusingly, our last show ever.[3] As such, we hired out the largest and grandest theatrical amphitheatre we could find and wheeled in the Marshall stacks.[4] No other band had ever even contemplated a rock show in this venue before - and that's exactly why we did it.

---

3 / To be fair, we didn't plan on this happening. After so many years of spending every waking second with each other, fighting over chord progressions one minute and dirty dishes the next, by the time our EP was done, we just wanted space from each other. As the legend goes, we never picked it up again.

4 / Marshall amplifiers are a staple of any fledging rockstar. You know you've made it when you have a handful of these guys on stage.

As we huddle together backstage staring at each other, a look of 'holy shit' slowly spreads across our faces as the screaming begins. Ten seconds goes by. And then another. And with each ten seconds, the noise of a sold-out room full of pubescent angst crammed up against the stage keeps surging in decibels.

But we're in no rush to move. Sure, there's more tension in making the crowd wait, but we're also being selfish. We're silently aware this is our goodbye, and we want to soak up the atmosphere as much as possible.

Then like a mythological creature summoned by the raucous of a room packed with adolescents, we walk back out, one by one onto the pitch black stage.

As I walk up to the mic stand and wrap my hands around my trusty Shure Beta 58A[5] to begin belting out our last song for our final show ever, I turn to my good friend and lead guitarist Matt, and say, *'Let's do this'*.

And this is it.

This moment right here.

As the hue of the yellow stage light fills my visual field, I count this among the top moments in my life. I open my mouth to sing, and I see for the first time, the crowd singing along with me.

It was surreal. People I had never met, singing the words I penned myself one random night in my bedroom. My art was their art. My passions, my thoughts, were theirs. This moment right here

---

5 / Shure Beta 58 mics are the Marshall stacks of singing. While a singer can't build an armoury of awesome guitars, effects and amps, we can still at least control what we sing into.

was the reason I wanted to become an artist. To let people experience what I had created.

FINANCIAL ADVICE

When someone asked me what I did for work, for many years I flinched at the words cascading from my mouth. And luckily so. If I had towed the line and got on with being a cog in the system, you wouldn't be holding this book in your hands right now.

"I'm a financial adviser".

The term financial adviser, on the surface, is a very simple idea: an adviser on financial matters. The problem is, with an overly complicated and outdated compliance regime, it's extremely time laborious to achieve a good outcome specific to each client.

The inconvenient truth of the financial advice industry is this: for the average consumer there is no chance of knowing whether purchasing financial advice will bring any value until they've paid the fee and received the advice document.

And there is a reason for this. Too many people are making too much money for the finance industry to change. The good news however, is a quiet subculture of Financial Advisers have splintered off, not interested in how things were, but interested in what they can be. What we are now seeing on the fringes of the industry, is people receiving life-changing advice. Not just on how to get the most out of their money, but how to get the most out of their life.

Being far more inspired to follow this beat of the drum, I set my mind to creating a service to manage my client's cash flow. What started out as an exercise in the benefits of positive restraint, blossomed into a full lifestyle and finance management framework centred around helping my clients discover what they wanted out of life, and how to use their money to achieve it. Or to summarise, how they could fund their ideal lifestyle.

Before we dive into the three-step process on how to achieve this outcome, let's have a look at the environment which prompted this type of advice to evolve, and why viewing personal finance in the same way now as twenty years ago fails to solve the problems of modern day life.

MODERN DAY LIFE

Wanting to learn more about my clients, I surveyed the twenty-five to forty-year-olds as to what they wanted out of life, and what they wanted to avoid. I expected the results to reflect everything I had ever read about Gen X and Y wanting to be rich, retire early on passive income, kick up the heels or go travelling around the world. The results, however, did not reflect that expectation.

Instead of early retirement, people wanted job satisfaction.

Instead of getting rich, people wanted more time.

Instead of perpetual travel people wanted something to show for their hard work.

I was amazed at the findings. Had I been lied to, or had no one simply done what I had done – gone to the demographic and asked? What I realised is that over the last twenty years, a lot has changed.

In fact, that is an understatement. Everything has changed.

The baby boomers grew up with parents from a war-torn era. They were taught that safety and security were purchased through the ownership of assets. And that's what the baby boomers did. They bought. From homes to cars to fancy appliances. Ownership represented security and freedom.

Gen Y, on the other hand, has grown up in an economy of exponential growth for the last twenty-five years. The concept of scarcity and the corresponding need to gather and own things has become an anachronism. Add in the boom of technology to facilitate the sharing economy, and we now have the concept of ownership moving from the domain of security to the realm of responsibility.

Why own a car when Uber can pick me up from anywhere I am and take me anywhere I want to go? I don't have to find parking, I don't have to own a depreciating asset, I don't even need to worry about sobriety. More convenience for a lower cost, where do I sign?

This idea of access over ownership has been a massive shift in the way we interact with the world. To that end, if you're under thirty, there's a good chance you're in the majority and no longer think you'll own property. Ownership takes time, it takes hard work, and it removes instant gratification[6].

And there is so much to be instantly gratified by these days. Whether you Tinder your way through the weekend, Netflix

---

6 / The historical argument for home ownership has been property grows in value over time. While this is still true, it is overly simplistic to say this is the best way to build wealth. Thankfully this book is filled with ways to build an asset base to provide you an income later in life whether you want to hold property or not.

binge your new favourite series or stream a new album on Spotify, whatever you want these days you can have it. Immediately.

The problem is, these new services come with a time cost. And despite the incredible complexity of our neocortex to create fully functioning and (mostly) rational humans, we still haven't outpaced our 200,000-year history. Simply put, our brain is not made to deal with so many things competing for our attention.

Even just a couple of hundred years ago there were few things to worry about: a) is there food, b) is there water, and c) is there shelter? If all three were checked, you were good. These days our tick boxes are a lot more complicated. Does your boss like you, did you choose the right career path, and is there kale in your green smoothie?

Our brains are so exhausted by these open loop questions that when you add the fact that we are working longer than ever, and filling every other second with a social media hit, it's no wonder we're under the pump – our brains no longer have time to relax.

But being constantly interrupted with distractions is modern day life, you can't avoid it. And saying 'let's go back to the old days when it was better' is redundant advice. Instead, you adapt and create shortcuts to get big results from little changes.

Research tells us all these distractions and interruptions creates a burden on us to make decisions. And each of these decisions saps you of your ability to make good decisions. It's called decision fatigue and explains why over the course of a day, your decisions get worse. Judges make worse decisions in the afternoon compared to the morning; people buy useless extras at car dealerships, and we are susceptible to 'impulse purchases' at the checkout. Therefore, the lower amount of decisions you make, the higher your ability to make good decisions.

So when the results of the survey I conducted came back, I realised what people needed wasn't just a budget to manage their money, but a system to manage modern day life. With so many things competing for our attention, how is it possible to make the best decisions? What I found was the more decisions were removed from the individual, the better the outcomes were being achieved in every area of life. From relationships, to career, to financial.

Once our minds are free from the pressure of having to handle every single distraction and interruption we end up making better decisions in every other area of our lives. By creating cognitive minimalism, we can start focusing on what we should be giving our attention to - performing better at our jobs, making time with family, and finding new experiences.

I don't know when my rent is paid, how much I have for my next holiday to New York, or whether my long-term asset base is getting larger, all I know is it is.

Now before we go any further, in order to understand why I have anything to say about lifestyle, you first have to understand my background.

SMALL TOWN BOY

Before my band of amateur rockstars and I descended upon the NSW Central Coast, we grew up in a tiny but beautiful coastal town of 6,000 people called Nambucca Heads.

Now when describing Nambucca Heads the most two common phrases are a) 'oh that place just south of Coffs Harbour', and b) 'never heard of it'. It's where old people go to die, young people escape to live, and middle age people who prefer to drive in the slow lane think they've hit the jackpot.

When you grow up in a small coastal town like Nambucca Heads,[7] there are a couple of sets of unspoken rules. The first set of rules is dictated by the kids themselves, and it goes like this: first rule is you *have* to surf.

If you don't surf, you have no social life. Period. The second is if you can't surf, you better be able to skate. Third is if you can't surf or skate, hang around in the background on a BMX bike. And absolutely no one rollerblades.

The other set of rules are dictated by the adults and goes something like this: 'you can be whatever you want'. So instead of real opportunity, hope gets delivered straight to the brain like some cranial IV drip.

I understand why. If you can't offer your children much by way of social advantages like the 'right' schools or the 'right' network, the next best thing you can do for them is build up their self-belief.

In one sense it's very sweet and beautiful. In the other, it's rather debilitating. Ultimate choice equals ultimate prison. The overwhelming pressure of unlimited choice requires skills a child or young adult don't have.

After many years of mulling over unlimited opportunity, I real-

7 / Or what my mother refers to as 'the end of the world'

ised how disenfranchising 'you can be whatever you want' really is. As Barry Schwartz's book *The Paradox of Choice* puts it, the more options you consider, the more buyer's regret you'll have, and the more opportunities you encounter, the less fulfilling your outcome will be.[8]

Being told you can be anything you want sounds amazing, but unlimited options without direction is an overdose of free will. Have you ever been in a situation where there were too many options, so you decided not to bother?

When the sheer amount of choices in life is 'anything you want', the most common and easiest response is often not to make a decision at all. Watching many of my friends growing up succumb to this pressure, I learned early on that any decision was better than no decision at all. You can always improve things as you get going, but you can't improve things if you never make any progress whatsoever.

MY INTERSECTION

All this brings me to my intersection of money and lifestyle. While everything I've done professionally over the last decade has to do with money, that's not what motivates me. I'm not a money guy; I'm actually a lifestyle guy.

Navigating the smorgasbord of options in life to come out with clarity is what I've been doing since I was a child growing up in Nambucca Heads, and living the care free lifestyle of an amateur

---

8 / Again, why I'm a massive believer in reducing decisions where possible and replacing non-crucial decisions with automation.

rock star into my early twenties has taught me a lot about the pleasures of achieving what you want out of life. But this book is not just about 'doing what you love'.

Typically books around enjoying a better lifestyle miss the giant elephant in the room. That is, what about your future? This book is designed to give you real-world, implementable solutions, so you don't end up with a massive credit card bill, or a lack of options in retirement.

This book is not about sticking your head in the clouds and ignoring your future financial life. Making sure your future is taken care of is just as important as enjoying yourself today. And of course, I want to achieve that with minimal effort, minimal decisions, and with all advantages afforded to me.

And will it include missing your daily coffee, or buying cheaper laundry powder? The answer is no. Unlike most people who speak on 'budgeting',[9] I have spent the last few years implementing this for my clients and have seen their outcomes. To get the best result from your money, know what you are working towards, and have automation do all the heavy lifting for you in the background without you having to think about it.

When I was sixteen, I wanted to be a rich rock star and live an awesome, exciting life. At twenty-two, I wanted to be a rich entrepreneur and live an awesome, exciting life. At thirty-two I realised it's not how much money I have, or how important my title was, what I really wanted, and what most people want, is to live

---

9 / I hate the word budgeting. It just seems so sterile and disempowering. How on earth is something called a 'budget' going to make my life better? It conjures memories of childhood rules and does not fit into my worldview of improving my life. For the same reason I hate the word 'savings'.

an awesome, exciting life.

That then is the story I wish to tell in this book. The idea you can ask yourself the right questions about what your ideal lifestyle looks like, and use the right tips on how to manage your cash flow, you too can learn how to decide what you want out of life, and how to go about funding it.

So having spent my entire life trying to figure out how to get the most out of it, and having a professional skill set devoted to the management of money, I decided to tackle the problem of modern day life by questioning these basic premises:

Is making a decision in life better than perpetually living in an open loop, even at the risk of not achieving the best outcome?

Does automating regular daily financial decisions reduce distractions and decision fatigue?

How can someone easily invest taking as many advantages possible with little to no knowledge?

So if you've stuck with me so far, my best bet is you are asking how you can achieve all of this. Great, let's get to it. The three-step framework centres around the three C's.

C is for Clarify.

Clarifying your ideal lifestyle is the first thing you have to do before you even start thinking about money. It replaces scatter-brain strategies such as 'make more money', or 'grow a property portfolio' with 'what is my purpose in life, and how can I spend more time working from there?' Once you have spent the time to understand yourself, you will have the direction you need to fund your ideal lifestyle now, and in the future.

C is for Cash flow.

Organising your cash flow replaces you at the centre of your financial life. It removes the premise that because you have the skills to make money, you have the skills to allocate it effectively. Go from over-spending to getting ahead with a strategy that can be implemented and automated within 24 hours.

C is for Capital.

Purchasing capital assets breaks the assumption of investing without a plan. It is written precisely to achieve what investing is meant to do, acquire the most money to pay yourself an income in retirement

We'll tackle the clichés around why people buy assets, whether it's because they have an emotional attachment to a type of investment, or because they think it's exciting. It is written to take advantages of the rule of law without taking on extra risk.

What does this book not cover? This book was not written to convince you to invest in any particular asset class like real estate, stocks, options or commodities. Speculating is a mug's game, and a mug I am not. You're fighting over scraps at the table with that kind of talk. And this book is not a secret code on how to travel the world while pulling in record numbers in cash.

What this book will do is give you the tools to take whatever situation you are in right now, and help you get the most out of it. Squeeze as much possibility and opportunity from it as possible. I've noticed, those with possibility and opportunity are not only happier but find themselves in better circumstances.

As such, this is my exposé on how to buy time, find new experiences, and keep more of what you worked for.

Let's do this.

EP 1
NIFY
TYLE

IF YOU DON'T KNOW HOW MUCH
YOU NEED, THE DEFAULT EASILY
BECOMES 'MORE.'

\- RYAN HOLIDAY

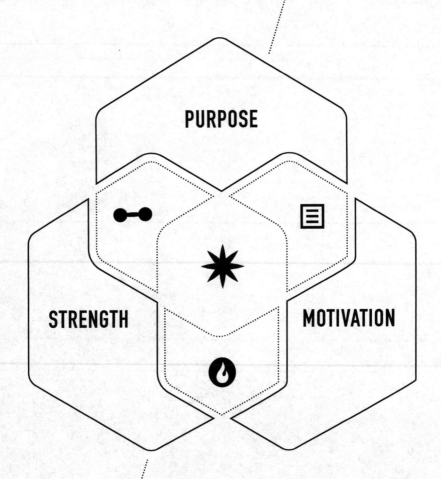

PURPOSE

STRENGTH

MOTIVATION

CLARIFY LIFESTYLE

Clarifying what you want out of life is the first step toward funding your ideal lifestyle. It's also the most important because it will have a significant effect on the rest of your decisions. The goal in life is not to accumulate more stuff and more money, but to hit the lifestyle, emotional, relational and experiential milestones you set for yourself.

Money is important, and we will get to that, but first things first, let's clarify what you want out of life and fit your money decisions in with those desired outcomes. Not the other way around.

ONE
THE CENTRE OF GRAVITY
YOUR PURPOSE

"IF A MAN KNOWS NOT TO WHICH PORT HE SAILS,
NO WIND IS FAVOURABLE."

– SENECA / *MORAL LETTERS TO LUCILIUS*

"IF YOU DON'T DESIGN YOUR OWN LIFE PLAN,
CHANCES ARE YOU'LL FALL INTO SOMEONE ELSE'S PLAN.

AND GUESS WHAT THEY HAVE PLANNED
FOR YOU? NOT MUCH.

– JIM ROHN

've spent ten thousand dollars to get my first session of leadership coaching, and Peter, the guy on the other side of the Skype call, has just floored me with his first question. He tells me I don't need to answer him straight away which is handy as I don't have one, and for the rest of the conversation, I'm doing my best to squirm out of having to find one.

You see, I recently realised I have a problem, and it's not one I ever thought I'd ever have. In fact, I'd never even heard of anyone else having this problem before which made it all the more embarrassing to admit it. But here it is: I've been aiming to work for myself for the last ten years, and now I've finally achieved it. I've hit the six-month mark in my business, and things couldn't be better. Great news, right? Not exactly.

I've run out of things to look forward to.

There's a common theme around attempting things, which says it's okay if you fail, as long as you keep trying. I'm sure you've heard it in one way or another. Samuel Becket put it as:

'Ever tried? Ever failed? No matter.

Try again. Fail again. Fail better'.

Every famous and successful person has their own iteration of this quote, and I have always loved it. It gives you the freedom to achieve without the burden of doing everything perfect from the onset.

But what happens when you reach what you are aiming for? What happens next when you don't fail? It's a question I never saw coming, yet it hit me straight between the eyes one morning on my way to work. I realised what I had been working towards for the last decade was now a reality, and I had no next steps.

As the prospect of simply accumulating more money for the sake of having more money was never a driving factor for me, beyond just 'keep doing more of the same thing' I felt lost at sea.

So I called around, found someone who could help me, and signed up on the spot. I needed this problem solved, and quickly. And as I loaded up Skype to speak with my new leadership coach Peter for the first time, I was not expecting to hear:

'What's your purpose in life?'

The moment his words rebounded off my inner ear and converted the sound to information recognisable by my frontal lobe I hated it. To be honest, it pissed me off a little. How dare he ask me this question? And how could I even begin to answer?

And if the idea of answering 'what's your purpose in life' is making you squirm in your seat as though I just offered you a shot of whiskey on a Sunday morning, I don't blame you. I felt the same way at first.

But once I had spent countless hours internally struggling with and ultimately solving this existential dilemma, it became one of my favourite questions to ask. It's an Everest that once conquered, will give you the greatest view of your entire life. A centre of gravity you can use to test all future decisions.

It isn't a religious question, so if your answer has to do with an afterlife you've missed the point. And the answer can't simply be 'to help people'. It's okay, though; that one was my first response too.

As Peter explained to me, everyone is in the business of helping people whether you're an accountant, an astronaut or an anaconda-hunting tour guide. We have to go a bit deeper on this if we're going to get anywhere.

Another reason this question is hard to answer is that it can't have anything to do with your career. For example, if you code apps for a living, it cannot be 'to create the best apps in the world'. We are not aiming for a professional mission statement; we are aiming a bit deeper than that also.

We are aiming for your purpose in life. The core of your passions. Your unwavering drive. The thing that given the chance, you would do better at than anyone else. And because it is such a hard question to ask, I'm going to help you out. I'm going to ask you three questions that will help you answer this big question.

It is an uncomfortable and audacious question, I know. Only compounded by the fact that once you spend the time necessary to articulate it, the implied next steps are you will now have the responsibility to yourself to do something about it.

With that in mind, I'd like you to take it seriously. For no other reason than you probably have never, nor will ever, do this again in your life. In fact we are happy to handle meaningless minutia for the rest of our lives just so we don't have to tackle this question. And even though you didn't expect this question, we're here now, so you may as well get comfortable and make the most out of it.

In my job, I saw day in day out, humanity's ability to ignore what is most important, for the busyness of day-to-day life. And it's heartbreaking to sit down with someone at the end of their career and go through these questions when it's almost too late. What's the point in finally being aware of what makes you tick when you're too old to do anything about it?

So I urge you. If you get nothing else from this book, do this exercise correctly. At the very least, you will have gained $10,000 worth of value for the price of a book. At the most, however, you will have this clarity for your entire life, and you will be able to test all future possibilities against this core value.

Here are the ground rules. I'm going to get you to grab your phone and hit record, and record at least two minutes of your streaming consciousness as you answer these questions. By far and away, the greatest use of 120 seconds of your life you could ever possibly imagine.

If you want to step up the effectiveness, just keep going. Don't stop at 120 seconds. Keep talking until you have explored each thought in your mind.

That's the weird thing about this exercise. We think we already know how we think. Re-read that last sentence – it's a strange sentence to write, but even weirder to comprehend. The truth is, most of us aren't brave enough to examine our life. We don't really know how we feel about these topics when they live on the peripherals of our brain. It's only when we give them the chance to take centre stage of our consciousness can we answer these hard question accurately.

It's already too late to turn back, so whether you are ready for this or not, you may as well go along with it. We are giving your purpose in life a one-time only chance of being the sole focus of your attention.

STEP 1 / CLARIFY LIFESTYLE

········ **EXERCISE 1.1** ········

Hit record on your phone and answer the following questions. Once you've finished, listen back and pick out the most articulate parts to write in this book.

....

Q *You somehow travel back in time and meet your family. You are there as a child, and your parents are in their thirties. What would you do, say, or otherwise influence them to change, which would massively improve their life?*

....

I'm not talking about warning them about upcoming illness or accident, or telling them to invest in Apple. I'm asking how you could improve the lives of you and your family. For example, I wish more than anything my family had access to easy to understand information to make their life better. This, by no coincidence, led me to realise my purpose is to help people achieve what they want out of life by simplifying information.

_____

_____

_____

_____

_____

_____

....

Q   *What happened in your life to make you feel so passionate*
    about this? Why is this the number one thing in your child-
    hood you wish you could change?

....

Don't look for the answer in a specific moment, as you will miss
the purpose of this exercise. For example, my number one thing
isn't 'don't tackle that massive guy on the school playground
and break every tendon in my shoulder to the point where you
pass out from pain', although that would be an excellent piece
of advice. Instead, mine is a general theme which is 'I grew up
in a family with lots of love but poor advice'. I wish there were
someone who could have mentored my family to achieve more.

_____

_____

_____

_____

_____

_____

_____

_____

_____

3   *What frustrates you about the world now that you wish you to change?*

Now we are taking these ideas and removing the emotional attachment. For as much as I want to prod your thinking with emotive questions, this isn't an exercise in masochism. So with the clarity of the last two questions let's now make it a bit more general. How could you make the world better, and what role do you play in that vision?

_____

_____

_____

_____

_____

_____

_____

Spend as long as you need on answering these questions by speaking into your phone. Then listen to your answers and pick out the best phrases to articulate how you feel.

Sometimes you will talk for minutes before getting to the answers you need. The point is to get this part of the brain moving. It's going to be a little rusty so don't rush it. And by no means do I expect you to be able to come up with the answer to the question of your purpose in life right now.

Hopefully, these three prompting questions get you thinking, but even with these answers don't put pressure on yourself to come up with your purpose in life straight away. If you think about it over the coming weeks, it will come to you, though. I've seen it many times before.

As long as your answer isn't just a surface response that could belong to anyone like 'my purpose in life is to help people', and it isn't to do with your career like 'be the best investment banker in Melbourne', we should be on track. Your answer should be as unique as your fingerprint. It is your 'why'. It is a deep well that would motivate you more than money.

Once you have answered this question, it's like turning on the windscreen wipers in the middle of a sudden downpour. You can see clearly. You can see where you're going, whether you are on course or not, and all of a sudden what was once blurry is now clear.

The rest of this book is predicated on the answer to this question, so while you're free to move on past this point with a general game plan, I challenge you to come back consistently to this question for *at least* the next couple of weeks until you are entirely satisfied with the answer.

SO TO THE POINT:

What is your purpose in life?

IMPORTANT IDEAS AREN'T COMFORTABLE

While I'm a massive fan of this question, I am very aware of its implication. Who on earth talks like this? It's not exactly good conversation material, is it?

When you meet someone they don't ask about your life purpose; you get asked about what you do for work. As a result, you have a well worn answer to that most boring of questions, but not a lot for what matters.

Another reason why most people never take this path of self-evaluation is that it's too easy to fill the void with noise, clutter, drama and distraction. And if there is any space whatsoever left over, we have media and advertising waiting there to fill any void happily.

And so our society tells us to be driven by results, flashy cars, by how far we can climb a corporate ladder. Why consider your deepest desires when your bonus is due to be paid next month?

But it's not hard to find stories of how the climb wasn't worth it, the view from the top was not what it was cracked up to be, and how given the chance to start over they would do it differently. Don't let that be you.

AVOID CHASING SHINY OBJECTS

In my experience, most people don't truly want to live off the grid and away from friends and family for extended periods of time. Many people find a lot of pleasure in working and achieving career goals.

The reason I'm not writing a book about leaving everything behind is because after six months on the road, I was burned out. Sure, slogging your life away in a job you don't connect with or believe in isn't a good idea, but aimlessly wander lusting around the world isn't the Holy Grail either.

In November 2010 I left Australia with a one-way ticket and no plans. After arriving in Chile, I drove through the salt flats, climbed Machu Picchu, and trekked through the Amazon jungle. I boated through Iguazu Falls, snuck out of Paraguay (long story),[10] partied my way through Buenos Aires, found an amazing hidden piece of paradise called Punta Del Diablo in Uruguay, and lapped up the beach in Brazil. I then flew to Europe, roamed through Amsterdam, more partying in Berlin, Barcelona and Nice, before spending a month in Antibes.

By mid-2011 I just wanted a routine. I wanted a timetable. I wanted a reason to be somewhere, anywhere. I had expired my ability to soak up new experiences and I wanted to pursue a worthwhile career again.

---

10 / Immigration officials confiscated mine and my buddies' passports, and we were left in purgatory on the Bolivia/Paraguay border. Long story short, we held a pretend public meeting where I had to apologise for being a dumb gringo and was given a three day emergency visa to get through Paraguay. However, we decided to stay longer and ended up in the mountains teaching English for a week with the Peace Corps. Problem was we would were never going to get through customs without more trouble, so our Peace Corps mates found us a locals only bus that travelled just over the border in to Argentina every day for grocery shopping. We paid the bus driver a small sum and smuggled ourselves across the border. Unbelievably we were able to get out of the country without a Paraguayan exit stamp. Winning.

KNOW THYSELF

The other advantage to knowing what your purpose in life is that you now have a target to hit. You now are no longer wandering through life aimlessly, disenchanted by endless options available to you, and exhausted from the decision to pursue an opportunity or not.

Once you have your purpose in life, will you be willing to sacrifice it for a higher salary? If Fight Club taught us anything besides the practice of splicing films, it's that 'advertising has us chasing cars and clothes, working jobs we hate so we can buy shit we don't need'. Thanks, Tyler Durden.

So, what is your purpose in life?

Stay on this question for as long as it takes. You can continue to read on past this chapter (I promise the rest is nowhere near this intense), but you need to be able to answer this question before you can piece together the rest of Section I of this book.

You don't have to find yourself on a mountain if you don't want to, but whatever you choose to do with your time moving forward, you'll be able to walk in the strength that only comes with knowing you are pursuing your purpose in life. And if you do choose to make a significant change, you will at least know why.

The final benefit to knowing your purpose is you will avoid burnout. I've worked with enough high-performing people to know that if you are crushing your soul by ignoring your purpose in life for long enough, your body will let you know.

The only remedy to burnout often is throwing everything away and starting again. We want to avoid that. Knowing what your purpose in life is, and organising your working life around it is by far the best long-term solution for high achievement without the burnout.

Once I understood my purpose in life was to make things as simple as possible for people so they could make decisions the best decisions for themselves, I ended up creating a financial advice service providing value to clients in a way I had never seen anyone else do. It even led me to write this book.

Figure out your purpose. It will contribute more to your internal strength and your long-term direction more than anything else you can do.

CHAPTER SUMMARY

Q How will this help fund my ideal lifestyle?

Knowing your purpose in life is the starting block. It will ensure you are focused on the right things. With an infinite choice of possibilities to do, achieve, and pursue in life, you can end up anywhere. You are going to spend your time doing something. If you don't pay attention to what fulfils you the most, you'll end up getting good at something you don't enjoy. And just because you are good at something, doesn't make it worthwhile

In the next chapter, we will begin adding additional blocks to discover how to best work according to your strengths. It is the best way to maximise the efficiency and effectiveness of your output.

Q How can I make it easy?

It's okay to read the whole book before coming back to this question, but once you have answered it, you'll be able to tailor the rest of the book to you.

Don't be in a rush to respond to this. It's a very profound question, which is why often it can help to think about moments or events that happened to you as a child.

It isn't a surface answer so 'helping people' is not sufficient; it's not a professional mission statement, so 'being the best at my job' is not good enough. We are looking for something deeper. The answer will be uniquely you.

TWO

PROFESSIONAL SUPER POWER

YOUR STRENGTHS

"TO DO A BETTER JOB, AND TO MAKE YOUR JOB BETTER,
WORK YOUR STRENGTHS."

– MARCUS BUCKINGHAM / *THE TRUTH ABOUT YOU*

"MOST MEN LEAD LIVES OF QUIET
DESPERATION AND GO TO THE GRAVE WITH
THE SONG STILL IN THEM."

– HENRY DAVID THOREAU / *CIVIL DISOBEDIENCE*
AND OTHER ESSAYS

The intense scream pierces our sleeping quarters like a hot knife through butter. A shot of adrenaline shoots through my body the moment those sounds snap me out of my sleep, and I'm brought back to life again. It's going to be a long six weeks.

I rip the bottom sheet off my bed and run to the hallway with more zeal than I knew I had available at 6 am. As I'm standing there, with forty or so other shaking and startled people, the assumed balance of power is concreted at that moment as one guy faints and no one waivers. None of us move.

During this quest of self-inspired torture, I put my mind and body through some of the most gruelling six weeks you can imagine. A night owl by nature, the 6 am wake ups every day were just the beginning. Breakfast, 20km run in the heat, lunch, crawl through mud, dinner, march in line till 10 pm. Shower. Sleep. Repeat.

A high school truant by trade, heading off to boot camp made no discernable sense whatsoever. My teenage years were mainly spent avoiding hard work and high grades with skills I thought were more appropriate at the time - namely surfing and singing in a rock band.

But in some type of masochistic lapse in survival instincts, I decided my laissez-faire approach to life wasn't setting me up for success, and I needed some self-discipline. And the most efficient way I figured of doing that was enrolling myself in the reserve army at age sixteen.

The government was desperate for enlistments so they took me. At sixteen I was old enough to die for my country, but not old enough to drink a beer. Go figure.

Needless to say as the only fresh-faced surfer of the lot, I'm about as incognito as a tin Jesus in a magnet factory.[11] Most of the recruits were there for one of two reasons, either they were out of employment options and in their mid-twenties or were dedicated career soldiers.

The differences aptly identified by one of the more aggressive youngsters in the platoon, when he put it simply as *'where else to you get paid to kill people?'*

And a long six weeks it was. I don't think I will ever be as drained as I was at that time. The day after I marched out, I spent an hour cutting away the blistered and calloused skin on my feet. You know your body disagrees with the punishment you've dished out to it when the soles of your feet start to shed en masse.

WEAKNESSES

And while I did learn a little bit about self-discipline, you don't have to be the revered and all-knowing oracle of high school life — a careers counsellor - to know this wasn't exactly playing to my strengths.

Though I learned firsthand the benefits of not working a job in which people scream in your face all day, I learned nothing there to leverage my natural abilities save for the skills of dressing up like Rambo and playing 'pow pow'.[12]

---

11 / I'm plagiarizing Russell Brand here in an attempt to sound intelligent. This was casually tweeted in 2009 by Russel Brand. To my knowledge never used again. Are you kidding me? That is hilarious. I'd love to own that idiom, however it's all @rustyrockets

12 / The universal name for child gunfights.

My lesson to stick to my strengths was only six weeks in the making, but I have seen people waste their life attempting to fill in their weak spots rather than play to their strengths. All this does is get you incremental improvements, and even those are probably fleeting.

But if you focus on improving your strengths, you're going to have accelerated learning. To put it simply, you're getting much better bang for your buck with your time by focusing on improving your strengths.

So why do we feel such a strong pull towards self-critique? Why do we all instinctively focus on our weaknesses more than our strengths?

If a child comes home from school every year with A's, and then one year turns up with a B, the typical first reaction is 'what happened here?' Or if you're performing well at your job and hitting all expected outcomes, your manager is still going to give you 'areas to improve on'.

It's because of the strong and long-lasting effect of negative emotions on the human mind. When we give negative feedback, we expect it to act as a deterrent or motivator for a longer period as we hold on to negative information more than positive information.[13] This natural phenomenon called 'Negative Bias' explains the powerful effect of shame accompanied by a reprimand at work, or a failed business venture.

And this all goes back to evolutionary biology and our primal

---

13 / Roy F. Baumeister, a professor of social psychology at Florida State University and author of the book "Bad Is Stronger Than Good," suggests four out of every five memories are negative.

brain. Mistakes were a matter of life and death for the majority of our evolution. If we missed a small movement in the grass, we were a predator's entree. If we failed to read the oncoming winter, we ran out of supplies.

Our entire bloodline, every single ancestor we have was good at survival and avoiding mistakes. Every single one of them reached mating age and successfully reproduced before their demise; it's implicit in you being here.

So we are selectively bred over millions of years to avoiding making mistakes. With that come strong feelings of shame and regret if we do. Thus working on improving our weaknesses has been fundamental to our survival and one of our most dominant natural inclinations.

However, this innate biological instruction does not serve us well anymore, as we no longer live in a 'kill or be killed' world. We won't be eaten if we make a mistake, and it's not our life on the line if we fail.

Don Clifton the Chairman and CEO of the Gallup Organisation and his team of researchers interviewed thousands of professionals to figure out what made the top performers stand out from the rest. Their conclusions were that the best performers always played to their strengths rather than focus on their weaknesses.

He completely disagrees with the idea that anyone can become competent in anything, or we should work on our weaknesses to get ahead. Instead, Clifton points out everyone has their unique set of talents and strengths and improving those will provide us with the greatest room for growth.[14]

While my stint in the Australian Reserve Army was a waste of time, I did learn something. I learned to play to my strengths, not my weaknesses. The final missing piece however was I still didn't know how actually to go about finding what my strengths were. Fast forward another decade and a half, and I finally do.

FIND YOUR STRENGTHS

So here we go. To find your strengths, take one part your purpose in life, and add one part your professional experience. Though this sounds terribly simple, if you don't understand your purpose, you'll never be able to play to your strengths. I'll give you an example.

As I've mentioned previously, my purpose in life is to make things simple so others can make the best decisions for themselves. So if I add my purpose to my professional experience with money, I work to my strengths when I simplify money so people can make the most out of their lives.

Knowing your purpose and working with your strengths isn't about getting all 'woo woo'[15], it's about being cognisant you can get good at anything with differing levels of success. Assuming no physical or mental limitations, this should be true for most people. Therefore rather than getting good at something, working with your strengths simply means you are purposeful in choosing what you get good at and expecting better results.

14 / Buckingham, M. & Clifton, D.O. (2001). *Now, discover your strengths: How to develop your talents and those of the people you manage.* London: Simon & Schuster.

15 / I equally love and hate this description for things that are a bit different.

It's an important point because, while you can get good at most things, you'll never get that extra edge unless you are working to your strengths. Your strengths are your day-to-day actions of implementing your purpose in the world.

The reason why people leave to find themselves on some 'never ending'[16] sojourn, only to come home a few months later, is purpose predicates action. In fact, it yearns for it. Once you know your purpose, you will want to enact it on the world.

Combining your purpose with your skill set is the best way to go about making sure you can bring about your purpose to the world. By knowing your purpose and using your skills to make it happen, you are playing to your strengths.

Ever wanted to be an expert in something? Take your purpose in life, and combine it with your profession. Your ability to find insights and give people new understandings will be far more effective than anything you've done before.

Ever wanted to feel steady strength and motivation to get up and go to work every day? Ever wanted the path of least resistance? Ever wanted to avoid wasting your potential? Avoid burnout? Ever wanted to get better results? Ever wanted to get through your work quicker? Ever wanted to find that endless reserve of enthusiasm?

I think you know where I'm going with this: understand your purpose in life, combine it with your professional skills, and play to your strengths.

---

16 / Never ending is normally around three months until the itinerant comes home broke.

EXERCISE 2.1

Q   *What is your purpose in life (chapter 1)?*

_____

_____

_____

_____

_____

_____

_____

_____

_____

Q   *What is your professional skill set?*

_____

_____

_____

_____

_____

_____

_____

_____

_____

....

Merge them together to find your professional super power –
your strengths.

....

_____

_____

_____

_____

_____

_____

_____

PLAY TO YOUR STRENGTHS

Now that you're aware of your strengths, you can go about re-directing your position in your company to best fit in with your strengths. And the best thing about it is, if you work for a large employer, you can probably start doing this straight away.

Getting a better-motivated, more productive employee who enjoys their job more is a no brainer for any business. You will have more energy; you will get better results, and ultimately make more money if you are working to your strengths.

If you are working for a small employer and see no chance of changing your position, then obviously that makes things a little harder. Job security is a major concern for most people, but I will say that the quicker you can play to your strengths in your job, the faster job security will become less of a problem.

If you are a business owner or entrepreneur, your ability to begin to carve out a niche with your insights makes perfect use of your strengths. With your own business, you have the control to move from a generic way of doing things, to a way that is uniquely you.[17]

Waking up in the morning and being able to anchor your work to your purpose in life, will give you infinitely more passion and drive to succeed. Working towards something bigger than a job description will improve your output immediately.

In fact, the overwhelming reason why the majority of people

---

17 / Commonly called a Unique Selling Proposition (USP) or Client Value Proposition (CVP), niching is both necessary to be successful in business, and best articulated by combining your passion with your professional experience.

waste a quarter of their day at work is that they are unchallenged, unsatisfied, and uninspired by their work. We need cohesion between purpose and day-to-day activities to feel engaged with our work. Increases in salary don't even motivate over the long term.[18]

Contrast this with merging your purpose with your professional experience. Your results, problem-solving ability, and willingness to succeed increase exponentially as your understanding and engagement with the topic far exceed your peers.

CREATE AN UNFAIR ADVANTAGE

If you start playing to your strengths, an additional benefit is you will become known for a particular insight, and you will start receiving attention. From there you can start getting priority on which projects you choose to work on, and the snowball gains momentum. It's one thing to be good at something; it's another thing to be known for it.

Your reputation, in turn, validates your worth to your employer. If you have ever wanted more bargaining chips for a promotion, a pay rise, flexible working arrangements or extended leave, then working to your strengths and becoming known for it is your ticket.

Conversely, if you don't play to your strengths, what happens then? Well, you'll continue to get the same results as you've always had. And if you are reading this book, I can assume you're not particularly interested in that. I can guess you want changes,

18 / *Forbes* article from September 2013, 'Who wastes the most time at work?' by Cheryl Conner

improvements, and some ideas on how to get there as succinctly as possible.

Playing to your strengths gives you the ability to leverage the new insights you now have about yourself from reading chapter one. And combining your purpose with your professional skills to create your strengths will give you direction in life.

Alternatively, you avoid playing to your strengths and keep working on the easy to identify weaknesses. But I've already covered what the experts have to say on that.

Then again, you may not have the confidence to go out and change your life to fit your purpose better. Perhaps you are a little nervous about making those changes, or you aren't confident you can achieve success?

If that is the case, I have a short sentence for you: Competence breeds confidence. Confidence comes from being competent. And how would you best go about being competent? That's right, working with your unique insights.

The day I started working from my purpose in life, I completely revolutionised my business. When I started my company mid-2013, I had no idea within twelve months I would create a service I hadn't even heard of, which in turn caused me to have many more discussions about lifestyle, which culminated in me writing this book.

As an ex-tax accountant, I knew cash was king, but I'd never seen advisers focus on this for the individual. Helping clients by not just tracking their spending, but moving around their cash to achieve what they wanted out of life was something I hadn't seen.

But once I knew my purpose and what my strengths were, this entire service sprang to life. And the minute I started doing this, I created a blue ocean for my business.[19] All of a sudden I was no longer competing on price or other benefits. I had moved my business to a highly valuable space in which other advisers were not involved.

What initially started out as a way for me to enact my purpose on to the world with what I do for everyday work, ended up becoming a lesson in competitive advantage. By discovering my purpose and combining it with my professional skill set, I created such a unique insight into the demands of my market I created a service with no known competitors.

And you can do this as an entrepreneur in a niche, or an employee bringing more value to your employer. Once you start playing to your strengths, your insights will soon breed a reputation.

Find more energy, be more efficient, and achieve greater results by playing to your strengths.

---

19 / If you're an entrepreneur, please read this book 'Blue Ocean Strategy' by W. Chan Kim and Renee Mauborgne. It's all about making your entire business model so unique you have no competitor.

CHAPTER SUMMARY

Q *How will this help fund my ideal lifestyle?*

By working with your strengths, you can enact your purpose in life. Your ability to provide unique insights to solve problems means you can validate your worth to your employer, or carve out a niche as an entrepreneur without competitors.

At this stage, your performance should go up as you stop wasting your time on trying to fix your weaknesses, which in turn should reduce stress, lessen the number of hours you need to work, increase job satisfaction and bring in more income.

Q *How can I make it easy?*

Knowing what your purpose is and combining it with your professional skill set is the easiest way to work towards your strengths.

Once you know what your strengths are, you will then need to move into this type of job description. Explaining to your employer you feel you can be of more value to the company by pivoting your roles and responsibilities should be seen as a valuable conversation from your employer. If not, you may need to look elsewhere.

If you are an entrepreneur, you will need to re-establish your position in the market by directing all your marketing to this message.

THREE

CATAPULTS KILL BUZZWORDS

YOUR MOTIVATION

"THERE'S A GUY INSIDE ME WHO WANTS TO LAY IN BED ALL DAY, AND WATCH CARTOONS AND OLD MOVIES. MY WHOLE LIFE IS A SERIES OF STRATAGEMS TO AVOID, AND OUTWIT, THAT GUY."

– ANTHONY BOURDAIN

"FEAR IS YOUR BEST FRIEND OR YOUR WORST ENEMY. IT'S LIKE FIRE. IF YOU CAN CONTROL IT, IT CAN COOK FOR YOU; IT CAN HEAT YOUR HOUSE. IF YOU CAN'T CONTROL IT, IT WILL BURN EVERYTHING AROUND YOU AND DESTROY YOU."

– MIKE TYSON

ou're lying in bed asleep, when an unfamiliar crackling sound and a heat that shouldn't be there begin to stir you. It's only when the smoke hits your nose you realise what's happening. Your house is on fire.

Your only exit is behind a door with smoke pouring out from underneath, and you're nearly out of breath as it is. Even though you had deadlines at work, errands to attend to, and emails to answer, the only thing on your brain right now is getting out of that house.

Priorities change pretty quick as an immediate threat to life becomes more apparent. Only, life is not just biological. It is also experiential. By that I mean, how you live your life is nearly as important as having life itself. The problem is, with a timeline of 80 years, we rarely face the immediacy of life.

Therefore, I have another tough question to throw at you: are you delaying your life? Are you pushing back the things you want to do because you believe you'll get there eventually? If so, the good news is there is a little-known exercise to change it all. But before we get to it, I want to explain to you what role motivation plays in helping you fund the ideal lifestyle, and why it's so hard to find.

YOUR RESERVE TANK

On your road to pursuing your purpose in life, there will be times when you will make mistakes, times when you don't feel like making the right decision, and other times when you don't even know how to stay on track.

Your motivation is your reserve tank to ensure you play to your strengths regardless of energy levels or if you have any idea of the next step. Unfortunately, motivation is hard to find.

This problem is the birth child of attempting to 'achieve goals'. The term itself, 'goal' is one of those horrible buzzword left over from the eighties. All now defunct, these late night infomercials sold motivation, hope, and dreams with a Billy Graham[20] zeal, and tried to motivate a generation to become motivated. But the truth was, once the hype of the latest conference wore back down, people went back to their normal lives.

Motivation isn't born out of pursuing a goal because pursuing a goal is not like escaping a burning house. Pursuing a goal is more like planning a trip to Bali.

Bali is nice. Flying to Bali would be a fun thing to do. In the future, one day, when you get on that plane, you will enjoy it. All these lovely things are great, but they are only niceties. They are nice to have. Motivation, on the other hand, is not considerate of 'nice to haves'. It is decisively binary. It either 'has', or 'has not'.

Psychologically, we are far more motivated to avoid pain, than we are to gain pleasure. Our motivation for escaping a burning house will always trump the goal of going to Bali.

That's the kind of motivation we want to harness. Your fear. This little-known principle is the key to your motivation. Chapter one is learning what your purpose in life is. Chapter two is putting your purpose into real-world implementable actions, and chapter three is harnessing your motivation to do something about it.

So let's get started on the exercise to discover your motivation.

---

20 / Billy Graham is the king pin of the modern day Christian Crusades. In his prime, he would travel all over the world, passionately declaring Christianity as the answer to life's problems.

FEAR AND DEATH

Imagine you're old and at the end of your life. Your weathered hands hold the rails of your favourite chair, as you steady yourself from the shakes plaguing you for the last five years.

It's another day of silence to look forward to, but you find solace in examining the familiar landscape you look out on to every day. As you lift a warm cup of tea up to your face, you contemplate your life. Are you happy with what you've done with your days or did you waste them?

Who do you see sitting there? Who have you become? What did you do with your life and what did you accomplish? What risks did you take, and did you end up following your purpose in life?

Now identify who you would hate to become. What type of person do you want to avoid becoming? Who would you hate more than anything to see seated on that chair? What would life look like if you considered it wasted? What should you have done differently? What did you fail to do? What didn't you change? What do you regret?

The real question is this:

Q *Who is the last person you would want to end up being?*

_____

_____

_____

_____

_____

_____

_____

Identifying who you would hate to be at the end of your life will be the greatest thing you can do to catapult you in the complete opposite direction with a ferocity you didn't know you were capable of having.

No longer will you have to depend on stirring up motivation, jumping up and down and rubbing your earlobes.[21] If you are clear on what you don't want to become, I promise you won't need a single piece of advice on motivation again.

And this is why. You know the risk of this fate becoming a reality. You probably know people like you want to avoid becoming, and you will do whatever it takes not to end up like them.

The secret comes down to two native and ancient drivers within

21 / A very peculiar exercise promoted by unlicensed wealth guru's to help 'attract wealth' from the BBC documentary 'Who Wants to be a Millionaire'.

all of us. Fear and death. If we combine the two, the fear of what you have become at your death, well then, you have an impressive set of internal combustion engines propelling you at full speed.

The field of psychology has already had their head wrapped around the idea of death as a motivator for some time, and have gone further to explain what we as a species end up doing with this motivation.

According to Terror Management Theory, we are all scared of death, but instead of using this fear to motivate us to achieve better outcomes for ourselves, we substitute this powerful motivator with adhering to cultural expectations.

These cultural expectations aren't all bad. They bond together communities who share similar values. We learn them from a young age. Our self-esteem in turn then directly links with how closely we align ourselves with and achieve these agreed upon values. Some of these rules are nice, some are confusing, and others are downright martyrdom.[22]

Once you're aware death can be a resourceful motivator that can be distracted with cultural expectations, the goal is to come back once again and judge everything through the filter of your purpose. Are you working towards what you want out of life or not? If not, use this exercise to kill the buzzword 'goal' and use this worst-case scenario to catapult you into motivation.

As your fears and motivations change and evolve with you as you mature as a person, you can tweak the course of your journey and give yourself new directions at any point. As you never set the

---

22 / Such as constantly being busy and living in stress, and giving a pound of flesh to your employer as a badge of honour.

final destination in stone, you avoid being overwhelmed by the pressure of choosing the best path in life. Rather, identify your purpose in life, work with your strengths, and use this technique to motivate you when uncertainties come.

The prospect of world peace couldn't stop world wars from happening, but the threat of nuclear war did.[23] It is the fear of the worst-case scenario that motivates the world to avoid violence as much as possible, not the goal of global harmony. Fear is the greatest motivator. Use it to your advantage

DISTRACTIONS AND CONSEQUENCES

Every week, without fail, I am asked how my business is going. The vast majority of the time, my answer is wrestled from me by an offering of a single solitary word. This word, ending with an upward inflexion, implies they already know the answer. This word, which I now disdain and consider the cancer of our modern-day lives, is 'busy'.

If I agree – 'yes, very busy' – I give off the impression that I am successful. Conversely, if I have an effective well-managed diary and answer 'no, not really' the assumption then must be I'm barely getting by. This thinking perpetuates the assumption that busyness is to be held in high esteem and never questions whether someone who is 'busy', is busy with the right things. If you're burning your time and effort in the name of being busy, what you really are is distracted.

23 / The father of the atomic bomb J. Robert Oppenheimer is credited with saving more lives than anyone else in history because of this.

If you ignore your purpose for long enough it will come out in other areas regardless.[24] Have you ever seen a middle-aged man with a bright new shiny car or a woman who leaves her family on a spiritual quest? Of course you have, we call it a midlife crisis.

These are examples people who realised they never spent the time to pursue their purpose in life, and the built up tension of not working to their strengths explodes in awkward ways. The worst part is, these distractions can't satisfy your purpose regardless. While being effective distractions they still do not solve the problem of failing to pay attention to your purpose and working towards your strengths.

PASSION IS NOT MOTIVATION

The day I sat down and thought about the worst-case scenario for the end of my life, I realised I didn't want to end up a small town person. With everything in me, I never wanted to be the guy who spent his whole life working an unfulfilling job, never travelling the world, or finding new experiences.

It became the mandate of my life against which I could easily measure any big decision. Any motivation I need is drummed up simply by imagining myself sitting on that porch with tea in hand, wondering why I never took the risk to improve my life.

Compare this exercise to the concept of following your passions. If following your passion created long-term motivation, there

24 / Castano, E., Leidner, B., Bonacossa, A., Nikkah, J., Perrulli, R., Spencer, B., Humphrey, N. (2011). *Ideology, fear of death, and death anxiety*. Journal of Political Psychology, 32(4), pp. 601-621.

would be millions more artists, creators, and musicians. However, I can tell you what you already know. Interests change, and passions wane.

So dedicating your life to a hobby is great when your name is Michael (whether Jordon, Jackson or Tyson). But if you're an adult and looking for motivation in your passions listen to The Edge,[25] 'It's a very unusual thing to be in a band like this. It's like being in a street gang. And it's all very well being in a street gang when you're 16, but it's bloody weird when you're 32.'

There's a reason why musicians get bored of playing music even if they love it, and there's a reason why chasing your passion is a bad idea. Your passion won't stay your passion forever. Unless you get to the very top of your field, choosing your avocation as your vocation will destroy that passion.

But the obvious risk is here, the chances of hitting the top are very small. So low it's not a plan, it's hope. It's like taking advice from a lottery winner saying 'sell all your assets now and buy tickets. It really works!'

Don't identify goals or even your passions. Instead, identify the last person you would want to become. This fear will catapult you into the opposite direction. And you'll be in for the ride of your life as you back yourself and pursue your ideal lifestyle.

---

25 / U2 guitarist, and a perfect example of someone following their passion in life for decades. I'm sure he still loves guitar, but like most musicians, you can tell he's rather exhausted with playing the same songs over and over.

MORE MONEY MORE PROBLEMS

Funding your ideal lifestyle is not a temporary philosophy; you're playing the long game. As such, staying motivated for the long haul is paramount to your success. Let's have a look at the consequences of not doing so.

What most people don't realise is a higher salary does not increase the chances of someone living their ideal lifestyle. In fact, pay rises generally result in 'lifestyle inflation', which leads to feeling trapped in a job, and the rat race has commenced.

And the consequences are constantly the same thing, working too much, failing to build long-term assets and failing to reach lifestyle plans. In other words, they waste their life.

Working too much is self-explanatory, but I want to give it some context. I'm a massive fan of working hard. In fact, I do not believe you can get anywhere without giving your pound of flesh once in your life. Whether you're building a business or a career, at some stage you are going to have to work harder than you thought you could to get ahead. Separate yourself from the herd.

But there comes a time when that pressure to perform at high octane should reduce as you get better at what you do. For example, I went from working eighty hours a week when I first started in financial advice, to working only eight hours a week once I had my own business set up with systems and employees.

But what happens when you start working a new role, with a higher salary than ever before? Well you are going to have less time for things that matter to you. Things like travelling the world or spending more time with your family. Maybe you have an entrepreneurial spark that you wish to flame but can't because you can never seem to find the time.

It is what I call the 'pay rise trap'. With each pay increase, your lifestyle costs inflate, and you become dependent on the new higher income. It's great until you realise you can't break yourself away.

At this stage, work becomes an immediate need to support your new level of lifestyle, and your pay rise is eaten up by new ongoing costs and you're trapped.

As the freedom you expected from a higher income dissipates, your stress levels increase as your entire life becomes about keeping the money coming in. Your choices reduce, you're unable to live in the present, and you end up at the worst possible place, distracted from your purpose and strengths to pay the bills.

But it doesn't have to be that way, and if you're already there, we can do something about it. That's coming up in Section II. What's important to know is that many others have been there too. It doesn't mean you have to stay there forever.

Once an expensive lifestyle matches your high income, you're stuck. You can't go anywhere. I know people who are stuck in jobs they don't like because they can't get $200k anywhere else. They would leave their jobs in a heartbeat but they can't. What they don't realise is it's not the income keeping them there; it's their expenses.

So what do they do? They fill in more time; keep the noise up, the distractions busy, the drama as full, and the expenses high just to drown out the feeling of being trapped. The ironic thing is, it's this exact lifestyle that keeps them there.

LOWER THE BARRIER TO SUCCESS

In addition to being a horrible motivator, articulating life goals will immediately place the barrier too high. The concept of choosing an ultimate destination for your life creates too much pressure to choose the best option. What if you choose the wrong destiny?

It makes the whole project too hard, too daunting. The pressure of making sure you pick *the best* possible outcome for yourself is too intense, and so we just end up avoiding the question altogether.

The smarter choice is to articulate what you don't want to be at the end of your life. It's a far easier exercise to conduct, and to find implementable strategies. You can nail that. You know exactly who you want to avoid becoming because you know what you hate.

Let the fear of becoming who you don't want to catapult you in the opposite direction. You don't have to know exactly where you are going, so the high barrier to success - picking the very best direction for your life - no longer has the power to keep you from making decisions. All you need to know is the exact person you don't want to end up as.

As time goes on, you can pivot in any direction you choose. As you learn or achieve new things, your views and opinions on what you want to be will change. And the best thing about articulating your fears is it works as a motivator regardless of where you're going. You can tweak your direction at any stage and still rely on your motivation to get you there.

Goals are useless. They're a hangover from the eighties that disenfranchised an entire generation. Don't live your life hoping to achieve goals. Kill the buzzword, identify your fears, and you will find yourself catapulted in the opposite direction with the G-force of a human centrifuge.

CHAPTER SUMMARY

Q *How will this help fund my ideal lifestyle?*

Articulating the last thing you want to end up as in life will ensure
with 100% accuracy you won't end up there. The clarity this exercise creates, ensures that you'll permanently store it in your brain.

The result, you will act. You will move. You won't sit silently on
this. Whenever a fork in the road appears, you will know which
one will take you further away from what you fear. And the further you are away from your worst outcome, the closer you will
be to your ideal lifestyle.

Q *How can I make it easy?*

Don't identify an exact end goal. It will create a high barrier to
success, as the pressure to pick the 'best' outcome for your life
is too overwhelming. Who is looking for that kind of pressure?

Instead, identify your fears to gain momentum to remove the inevitable uncertainties we all face. You will have more motivation
to take on challenges, as you will do anything to avoid becoming
what you know you do not want to be.

FOUR

SPICED UP PIRANHAS

A THOUGHT FOR TODAY

"WHAT DAY IS IT?" ASKED POOH.
"IT'S TODAY!" SQUEAKED PIGLET.
"MY FAVOURITE DAY," SAID POOH.

– A.A. MILNE

"THERE HAS TO BE SOME FORM OF
PUNCTUATION, OR LIFE JUST SEEMS
UTTERLY RELENTLESS."

– RUSSELL BRAND / *MY BOOKY WOOK*

Are there piranhas in there?'

'Yeah.'

'So…we aren't swimming in there are we?'

'Yeah.'

'Wait. Yeah as in, yeah we *aren't* swimming in there, or yeah as in we *are* swimming in there?'

'You can swim.'

'With the piranhas?'

'Yeah.'

I'm sitting in a poorly painted but beautifully made long wooden canoe, a day's boat ride into the middle of the Amazon River. I'm with two of my best mates, and I'm struggling to figure out whether our guide is insane or not.

He's already tracked down and jumped on a massive anaconda in the grass (I've seen the movie, and I'm not touching that). He led us into a crocodile ambush (Usain Bolt had nothing on me). And now he's staring at me with a calm assuredness across his face, telling me one of two things. Either a) he's never lost a single gringo to these terrifying gilled carnivores, or b) he's lost many and just doesn't give a damn.

Screw it. I'm going in anyway.

I didn't take a flight on the most precarious of small planes over mountain ranges of thick jungle, climb into a rickety old boat,

4 SPICED UP PIRANHAS / A THOUGHT FOR TODAY

float down the Amazon for a day and avoid being eaten by giant reptiles, only to be bullied by miniature marine monsters.

So I jump in. And as my bravado hits stratospheric levels, I realise piranhas don't like their meat still twitching. They'll rip apart a dead carcass, but can't be bothered much by the prospect of a fight. You can still swim, but I don't recommend floating. As you could imagine, every appendage was on max rotate.

Ironically, I ended the day with the hunter becoming the hunted as I baited up some hooks and started fishing. When I eventually pulled one of the little buggers out of the water, I remember feeling a small pang of guilt. As I held his little vicious red, white, and black body in my hands, I whispered 'thanks for not eating me'.

Obviously, I didn't extend him the same courtesy and felt very comfortable later that night with my place at the apex of the food chain while picking the white flesh from his little piranha bones. We spiced him up good and fried him up over a fire. Good eating really.

And there I was. In the middle of the Amazon jungle, no phone reception, no errands to chase up, no emails to check, rocking back and forth in a hammock, with nothing else to think about besides the sounds of the Amazon. I was as present as I could possibly be, and it was awesome.

THE MONEY/TIME QUADRANT

Do you remember back when you were a youngster running around with all the time in the world but not a cent to your name?

This glorious and rather limited lifestyle phase is what I call the All Time No Money Quadrant.

Oh, how things change.

You finished school, maybe had a part time job, probably ended up at university, and all of a sudden you didn't have the same amount of time anymore. At least you were making good money right? Well not quite. It was early in your career, and you probably didn't have any money either. Now you were in the dreaded No Time No Money Quadrant.

All was not lost though as then you perhaps put in a few years of hard work, rose through the ranks or built a successful business, and now you had 'money'. Not all the money in the world, but enough to pay the bills and some left over. You had enough to do what you wanted. Well almost. You would have if not for all the commitments and responsibilities you now had to fit into your weekends. Welcome to the No Time With Money Quadrant.

If only we could go back in time and ration out the extra time we had while we were younger, with the extra money we have when we are older.

Except we're not mates with Doc and Marty[26] and time travel is not a viable option. And so we are left with two choices.

Promote the idea that busyness is a goal in and of itself. Hold it as a badge of honour as if the action of being under the pump was an accurate indicator of progress. Don't think too much about never having enough time to enjoy yourself, and keep up the busyness facade.

---

26 / For those not up to date with *Back to the Future* folklore, these are our main two protagonists of the movie.

Avoid the trap of being busy and figure out a way to find that elusive Time With Money Quadrant.

Busyness creates a drop in performance in all other areas. It's the classic spinning plates analogy. There are only so many you can spin until they all start falling.

The main problem of coming to terms with busyness is there have been very few implementable strategies on how to avoid being busy. It's often centred on being better with 'time management'.

Telling someone who's busy to be better with time management is like pushing water uphill with a rake. Firstly, thanks for your insights enlightened one. And secondly, put down that gardening tool, you impress no one with your redundant landscaping skills.

Dealing with busyness in modern day life has to be approached with particular nuances with which the generations before Generation Y have little experience. There is officially too much to deal with in a 24-hour period, so the only option is to outsource to automation.

Automating not only frees up your time but much more importantly frees up your mind. In turn, it creates a knock on effect, a snowball of better performance that frees you more time.

From dealing with successful and busy people over the last few years, I've found the best way to find more time is to get better at what you do for work. Not just be better with 'time management', but to work with your strengths to get better results for less ongoing effort. The next step is to free up your headspace by outsourcing to automation.

So what can you automate?

What about relationships? Now, excluding those times when you would *prefer* to outsource your relationship to someone else, the idea of letting someone else take your partner out for a date and some extra-curricular activities probably doesn't sit too well with you. As such, I wouldn't recommend automating your relationships.

What about your job? I've read stories of people achieving this, so unlike relationships, it appears there is some room for success – though I'm not sure your boss would like it too much. Hiring a lookalike is probably more expensive than you think, and what if they ruin that classy reputation you've built up since the small disaster at last year's work Christmas party?

There is a chance you can change nothing, and simply force your brain to achieve better results. From research and anecdotal evidence, may I suggest one of two popular options? Get drunk. Or meditate every day. Both bring stillness to the mind but do differ in long-term health benefits.

So if after examining the other options you decide none of these applies to you, then outsource the biggest source of stress, your finances. Most notably your cash flow.

Ultimately the less you have to think about, the more you can concentrate on working with your strengths, increasing your output, reducing the amount of time needed to achieve, and thus giving you more time to spend on things that matter.

THE PROBLEM OF MODERN DAY LIFE

Your mind was originally equipped to perform now-redundant skills. You know where you can find water, food and shelter. You're at a very low risk of being eaten by a predator. But now your mind battles with modern-day problems infinitely more complex than your ancestor's brain was built to manage.

Your simple physiological requirements have been replaced by an endless array of choices, information, advertising and modern-day living. And with our ability for boredom completely eradicated with the advent of smartphones, we are now constantly stimulated and no longer have mental down time. No matter where you go, your digital leash follows.

As a result, studies show that we are 'present' only half our lives.[27] We spend the other half lamenting the past or planning for the future. The interesting revelation from these studies shows it's only when we have the ability to be present we are happy. That's why reducing the clutter of your mind and identifying what you want out of life on a daily basis is so important.

Your mind is a thinking machine, that's what it was built to do. But with its default setting akin to a prized race hound sprinting out of the gate, the problem with modern day life is there is no chance for pause.

Modern day life requires you to deal with decisions all day every day, so articulating what you want out of life and automating the funds to turn up each week without having to think about it reduces the amount of decisions you have to make, which in turn improves every other decision you make.

27 / Killingsworth, M. and Gilbert, D. T. 2010, *"A wandering mind is an unhappy mind"*, Science, Vol. 330 no. 6006, p.932

GUILT-FREE POCKET MONEY FRIVOLITY

A massive part of living in the present is to be able to spend money in the present, although we all have a differing view of how much that should be. As such, one of the best ways you can ensure you are allocating a good amount to the present is to pay yourself pocket money on a weekly basis for you to spend guilt free.

The reason why I think it is so important is that a) we make around ten financial decisions a day, and this strategy reduces the chances of over-spending on account of decision fatigue, and b) it ensures you actually get out of the house and spend. Obviously dichotomous answers, but they have the same result, ensuring you enjoy today without going overboard.

From research[28] and experience, it's been fascinating over time to realise people are more or less evenly spread (give or take a percentage or two) across one of four categories. We are all either savers or spenders, and then we are either heavy or moderate versions of each.

First, are the heavy spenders. These are the types that will spend more than what they'll earn and will have anywhere between twenty thousand to two hundred thousand dollars in personal loans and credit card debt. It isn't so much they don't realise they fit in this category; it's more they don't care, or find it too difficult to fix. They generally stay in perpetual debt for decades.

Second are the moderate spenders. These will spend everything they earn, but won't go overboard into a spiral of debt. These people don't throw caution to the wind as they have the discipline

28 / https://www.moneysmart.gov.au/managing-your-money/saving/how-austra-
lians-save-money

not to get into life-altering debt, but they are more interested in a new toy than the prospect of buying a new home. They will have around five thousand dollars in credit card debt from a holiday they slowly pay off – at which point it's time for another holiday.

Third, we have the moderate savers who will save money, but not for long-term wealth creation. They want to go to Rome in six months, but they don't believe in using credit cards. So they will save the money themselves and spend it overseas. These type of people are interested in starting an investment portfolio but don't know where to start so they keep waiting for the right time to get into the market, which they invariably don't.

Lastly, there are the over-savers. This type of person will use a tea bag twice, laugh at anyone with an unused gym contract as 'it's a waste of money', and view the world through a filter of debits and credits. They probably have investments regardless of the size of their income and put as much aside as possible for savings. Absolutely no personal debt, and don't expect a beer in return if you're on rounds.

Which one do you identify with? If you're a heavy spender you have some hard decisions to make, and if you're an over-saver, it's okay to go out and enjoy your life today, you don't have to spend your life planning for tomorrow.

By having an amount automatically put aside for you each week, it ensures you have a handy sum to spend on living in the moment each week with people who energise you, doing things that allow you to be in the present. All the while keeping you in check to what you can reasonably afford. And the best part is, you will know this is guilt-free money to spend without having to consider anything else.

ANTIQUITY INFLUENCES

The story of Icarus is one of my favourites. In fact, Hercules himself enjoyed it so much he built Icarus' tomb to commemorate it. Let me share it with you.

A talented Athenian craftsman named Daedalus was commissioned by the king of Crete to build the infamous Labyrinth to imprison the Minotaur (told you it was a cool story). His son Icarus came along for the ride.

Long story short, Daedalus and Icarus are imprisoned on the island. They can't escape by boat, so the ever-industrious Daedalus builds two sets of wings from feathers and wax, and tells Icarus they can fly to freedom.

Now, during this one and only human ornithological event in history, there are two rules: you can't fly too low, or the sea spray will soak the feathers, and you can't fly too high, or the sun will melt the wax. But there is a pocket, a Goldilocks zone through which they can fly to freedom.

All is good for the majority of the flight, until the brash young Icarus soars too high into the sky, melts the wax holding the feathers together and plunges into the sea to his death.

The story has been told over the last few thousands of years as an example of what happens when you push a good thing too far. Icarus, our young and ambitious yet flawed hero, loses his self-control and is snuffed out in a blaze of glory.

Learning how to put the appropriate amount of money aside each week to spend on enjoying your life today so you don't have to think about it is not a skill many people master. Instead, spending is left up to the strength of your self-control and becomes a constant drain on your decision-making ability.

Either focusing too much on today and over-spending or constantly living in the future and over saving has to be two of the most prominent mistakes I see people make on a regular basis. I very rarely meet people who manage to get this right.

Epicurus[29] on the other hand, spent his life putting forward this message of balance. An ancient Greek from the Hellenistic era, he started a community in a garden outside the city walls of Athens. Life was devoted to finding joy in the moment without needing excessive amounts of 'stuff'.

He was the first Western philosopher to diagnose the issue of insatiability. It was a widely popular[30] philosophy for its outlook of valuing the art of living over the unrelenting pursuit of 'more'.

His teachings centred on the idea of taking pleasure in simple things rather than chasing more pleasure in more things. He taught that insatiability was the undoing of the individual and that it was better instead to be happy in the moment, to stop postponing joy, and to focus on one's physical and mental health.

This philosophy reflects the Eastern traditions of meditation and recent Western psychology showing the benefits of being in control your mind. And the easiest way to be in control of your mind is by outsourcing your decisions to automation. Constantly relying on self-control is a poor use of your daily decision making ability.

29 / An actual real person this time.

30 / Images of Epicurus outnumber any other philosopher in antiquity.

So the easiest way to achieve your ideal lifestyle on a daily basis is first to articulate it, and then filter out an amount needed to reach it every week.

In this next exercise, I'd like to spend a bit of time figuring out what you would like to do on a day-to-day basis. We have uncovered your purpose and how to work towards with your strengths, we've discovered your motivation, now it's time to decide what your personal pursuits should be.

With so many distractions willing to take up your time, articulating what an ideal week looks like will enable you to make sure you're also spending time doing what you love on a regular basis.

·········· EXERCISE 4.1 ··········

Write down what an ideal lifestyle looks like to you. What's your weekly bucket list? It doesn't have to be massive, and we are going to space it out over different time periods from what you would like to do daily, to once a week. Here we go.

Q   *What would you like to be able to do every day? Cost?*

_____

_____

_____

_____

_____

_____

_____

_____

_____

_____

_____

_____

Q   *What would you like to do once a week? Cost?*

_____

_____

_____

_____

_____

_____

_____

_____

_____

_____

Now you know what an ideal lifestyle looks like on a daily basis, in Section II we will look to make sure you can afford to filter this amount of money on an ongoing basis. Our goal is to ensure you have an amount to spend each week guilt-free while simultaneously paying your bills and building long term assets.

CHAPTER SUMMARY

Q *How this helps fund your ideal lifestyle?*

The previous three chapters gave you specific tactics on how to put your life on a course to achieve your ideal lifestyle. This chapter is making sure you don't spend your entire life planning, but also to live in the moment by having new experiences and enjoying life on a daily basis.

You achieve this by articulating what your ideal lifestyle looks like on a week to week basis, and by setting aside an amount each week to spend guilt-free in order to achieve it. This gives you the freedom to enjoy your life without being like Icarus and going overboard, or without relying on your self-control to make financial decisions every day.

By making the decision upfront as to what you want out of life each week, and organising an automatic amount to turn up each week to fund it, this won't affect your cognitive minimalism or go on to cause decision fatigue.

Q *How to make this easy?*

Articulating your ideal lifestyle is half the challenge. Having automatic payments moving money around in the background to a separate spending account for you to achieve this lifestyle on a day-to-day basis is the other half. We cover more on that in Section II.

FIVE

ASSETS AND AGING

A THOUGHT FOR TOMORROW

"LIVE AS THOUGH YOU DIE TOMORROW,
LEARN AS IF YOU LIVE FOREVER."

- MAHATMA GANDHI

✈

"SET YOUR MIND ON A DEFINITE GOAL AND
OBSERVE HOW QUICKLY THE WORLD STANDS ASIDE
TO LET YOU PASS."

- NAPOLEON HILL, *THINK AND GROW RICH*

t's mid-2011, 10 am, and I'm lying on the beach at Antibes on the French Riviera. I've been doing this every day for a month, and I could easily do it for another.

I'm meant to be looking for a job, but the idea of scrubbing the Dilbar[31] like my mates seems to be far less fun than working on my tan. Problem is, I'm running out of money.

This most pivotal of problems gets solved however when I receive an email from Captain Charlie of the 62-foot yacht, Crystal Clear. He says I've got a job waiting for me, and to fly back over the other side of the world to the Caribbean.

We Skype, and he gives me the full job description. While not sailing, I would take guests for treks over the islands before cooking dinner on a beach fire. I would use my finer skills picked up from my music days to play for them during the evening, all the while perfecting my Spanish, as Charlie is an Argentine.

And as I sat on my bed on Millionaire's Lane[32] having this Skype conversation, I realised this was the best job I could ever ask for. Learning to sail, exploring tropical islands, playing music, and perfecting my Spanish. Where do I sign?

We make plans for me to fly home to Australia, say goodbye to my parents again (this time for a couple of years) and sail off into the sunset to pursue my new life.

Except I never jumped on that second flight. I stayed in Australia,

31 / A massive 110-meter super yacht docked at Antibes owned by the richest man in Russia, Alisher Usmanov.

32 / *Millionaire's Lane* was an ironic term. I was living in a holiday park at the time, and Millionaire's Lane was where all the 'fancy' places were. By fancy I think it meant the toilet worked.

and told Charlie I was never coming. Why? Why on earth would I give up such an amazing experience?

Because despite it being an awesome opportunity, it would only have been awesome for my ideal lifestyle that day. It was a horrible choice for my ideal lifestyle in the future. And the thing about your future is, it lasts a whole lot longer than your today.

YOUR IDEAL FUTURE

Funding your ideal lifestyle today is about deciding what you want out of life, and allocating your cash flow to meet it. Ensuring your future is looked after means putting aside small amounts of money regularly, purchasing investments, building the largest sum of money possible, and drawing down on that asset base to provide you an income when you no longer work.

In my experience, deciding what you want out of life in the short term is difficult, but still achievable. Deciding what you want out of life over the long term, on the other hand, is impossible.

The reason being, you change so much over the course of your lifetime. What you hold valuable now will probably change in thirty years. Therefore, while an exercise in deciding what you want out of life is appropriate for short term plans, the same can't be said for long term plans.

Instead what we will aim to do is to figure out how much you will need to be 'comfortable' in retirement. In this way, we can make sure you are prepared to be able to live your ideal lifestyle in the future, whatever you decide it should look like at that stage.

····· EXERCISE 5.1 - YOUR COMFORT AMOUNT ·····

This calculation is quite simply 70% of your salary today.

YOUR SALARY: _____ **X 70%**

= YOUR COMFORT AMOUNT

This comfort amount is now what you should be aiming for as income for when you no longer work. And all of that is well and good, but how do you know how much of a capital base is required to receive this much income per year?

This brings me to the second calculation. Research tells us if you are drawing down 5% of your money each year, it should last over a long period because the long-term average of growth investments is around 7.5%.

The theory goes, if you only draw down 5%, then the remaining 2.5% can be used to fight against inflation. It isn't perfect mathematics, but it's a pretty good rule of thumb.

············ EXERCISE 5.2 - YOUR CAPITAL BASE ············

Your capital base = Your comfort amount / 5%

Your capital base =

Over the course of my personal finance career, I have a particular insight that I feel is important to share here. That is, the older you get, the more money matters to you.

When we are young, money isn't everything. I'm sure you have great memories of times when you spent no money at all. But this changes over time. Whatever your dependence on money is right now, double it, and that's how important you'll consider money to be later in life.

I think it's because, over time as people become less tolerant of risk and focus more on being comfortable, money provides an efficient way of providing both. Add on the fact that, at some stage, you will no longer be bringing in income, and we have a strange juncture where money means more than it ever has while at the same time your ability to bring more in ceases.

So funding your ideal lifestyle in the future is less about deciding what you want it to look like, and more about focusing on creating a situation where you can receive a regular amount coming in each week to ensure you remain at a comfortable standard of living.

When you eventually get to the point that you are no longer working, you can plan your ideal lifestyle at that stage. But your focus now should be ensuring you build up a large enough sum of money to fund those decisions in the future.

PURPOSE OF INVESTING

"I have $50,000, and I want to invest."

"What for?"

"I think I can make more money."

"What's your timeline?"

"A couple of days."

"Don't."

For as much as I consider helping people decide what they want out of life, and organising their cash flow to meet those plans to be the most valuable part of this book, I also know what will save you the most money: learning what type of behaviour to avoid.

It's has nothing to do with only buying groceries on discount, or moving your banking across to a new bank because of marketing gimmick on refunding 1% of all purchases.

It's simply this: know why you're investing.

The reason I say know why you're investing as a top priority is because once you understand why you're doing it you will be able to make better investment decisions moving forward.

And even though I will say this countless times through the book, I'm going to spend a little time explaining why the purpose of investing is not to make more money in the short term, but to provide you an income later in life when you no longer work.

The reason I say don't invest trying to make more money in the short to medium term is that no matter how much you try, you are going to be emotionally involved with the outcome of the investment.

It's going to be something you think about, something that distracts you from your ability to perform at 100% in other areas of your life that are more important to you such as doing well in your career, spending time with your family and friends, and downtime to enjoy yourself.

The reason I know this is because I've seen it happen time and time again. You're going to care about the outcome; you're going to spend time thinking about it. I know you will. You will want to 'win'. You will want to be smarter than the market. You will want 'more money' and will see it as 'free money' if you wake up one day richer than the day before without working for it. You will consider yourself an 'investor' and all the sexy connotations that come with it. You would have heard people making money from 'hot tips', and you will want to get in on all of this.

And the truth is, let's say you're in the lucky 50%, and after all this emotional and mental involvement, reducing your cognitive minimalism and affecting every other area of your life...let's say you make 20%.

Who cares?

I can almost guarantee it's going to be an almost pointless amount of money. The reason I know this is because only self-made people who didn't grow up with a lot of money make this investment mistake. The reason is, if you have arrived at a point in your life where you have been successful enough to pull together a little bit of money to invest, it's easy to think that kind of success will follow you into the investment market.

But it's a half-baked idea. Yes, real wealth is made with investing, but we are talking much bigger numbers over a much longer time frame.

If you're in a position where a drop of 20% in the market scares you – you shouldn't be in there. You have too much riding on the success of the investment. Truth is the people who make the most from investing make it when the markets radically drop. Don't get me wrong; they lose money too, but they buy up. Everything. They buy everything at outrageous discounts. And the reason they do that is because they can afford to.

These investors don't need the money. They can lose millions of dollars in a week, and it doesn't matter. They know two things: a) unless the entire economic system around the world fails, the market will go up again, and b) if they buy now, they buy at a discount.

This is true investing. Holding for the long term, and buying in the dips. It's not rocket science, but now you know the method real money is made via investing and how the rich get richer.

Investing small amounts of money here and there for short amounts of time because you 'want to do something' with your money and hope to make an extra 20% over the course of a few days/weeks/years doesn't do much for real long term wealth.

So yes, the rich get richer from investing, but it's a very different type of investing then what the majority of people can do. Therefore I stand by my point for the 50% chance of earning a relatively small amount of money at the cost of decision fatigue is not worth it.

So while it is possible to earn money over the short and medium term with investing, it's simply not worth the mental cost and effort. Next, I will explain to you the two high probability, low emotional attachment ways of investing – cash for short term and 'out of sight out of mind' for long term.

THE LONG AND THE SHORT OF IT

Short term is very easy to understand. Hold your money in cash until you need it. Makes sense as there is essentially a 100% chance of knowing exactly how much money you will have at a particular time in the future. Let's see examples of this type of investing.

If you want to go travelling, you'll probably want the money in less than 12 months. In that case, hold the money in cash. If you plan on buying a property in five years, hold your money in cash. Again, you will know how much you are going to pull out for your deposit. Considering the high risk of losing your money, and the effects of decision fatigue as you become highly emotionally involved in the outcome, short-term investing is not worth it.

Now to the real investing, the type of investing whose sole purpose is to provide you income when you no longer work: long term investing.

Long-term investing has statistically a far higher chance of succeeding. If you consider the market is simply a broad term for all the largest companies in the world, do you think the biggest companies in the world will be bigger or smaller twenty years from now?

The global population will be larger. The global supply of money is getting larger. The amount of middle class with access to this money is growing larger. Companies are getting better at offering products and services people want, and they are getting better at making a profit.

If I were to take a stab at it, I'd say there is a 99% chance this will happen. And if it does, then the stock market will reflect this. As such, by investing over the long term, your chances of success hugely improve from 50% up to 99%.

Secondly, you don't want to have to think about it. As there is no emotional or ego attachment to an investment twenty years from now, it's not something you have to think about – at all. As the time frame is so far away with the knowledge there will be many ups and downs, you won't be highly emotionally attached or distracted having this money invested in the market. And the best way to achieve this is to automatically filter off small regular amounts of money to an investment you don't ever have to think about.

We will get to what you should be investing in future chapters, but at this stage the biggest benefits of long-term investing are: a) I don't have to think about it, b) it will be low cost, so I don't lose my profits over many years, and c) it's in a low tax environment, so I get additional risk-free bonuses over many years. The total effect of this low input and low cost/low tax investment strategy over twenty or thirty years is substantial.

If the quality of your ideal lifestyle in the future is directly affected by the size of your long-term investments, then you should focus on building an investment system to build a large asset base in the most efficient and effective manner.

COGNITIVE MINIMALIST INVESTING

The idea of cognitive minimalism is to push as many decisions as possible to automation and technology and to focus on what's important to the individual. Doing so helps reduce decision fatigue, which in turn improves every other area of life.

The reason why investing gets a specific mention when we're talking about fostering an uncluttered mind is that I've seen it take up huge amounts of head space.

As I said above, investing for the short and medium term is redundant. Less than five years you have a 50% chance of making money, and you're more than likely to change medium term goals as situations and opinions change over time.

Long-term investing, on the other hand, is the best way to invest. And while if you moved all your investment decisions to long-term it would be a great start, you still want to avoid needing to play a role in the ongoing management of the investments.

Therefore, if you are investing in property ensure you have a great property management company looking after you. And if you are investing in the stock market, ensure you're diversified across many companies to ride the long-term upward trajectory.

What this specifically means is are you looking to 'flip' properties? If so, this is going to take a lot of your concentration. Or are you constantly buying and selling different stocks? If so, are you really beating the benchmark[33] of a low-cost indice ETF?

---

33 / The benchmark is considered investing in broad market indices. This means indiscriminately investing across all the biggest companies instead of picking and choosing specific investments.

Again, these are perfectly fine ways to make investment returns, but the additional cost of reduced performance in every other area of your life due to decision fatigue simply makes it not worthwhile.

Of course, there are always exceptions to the rule. For example, if you are someone who has spent their career buying and selling houses for themselves and others as a Buyers Agent – obviously as an expert and your day-to-day job – it's completely fine to be overly active and interested in the area. It is no longer a distraction at that stage; it is a profession.

If however you are not a property or equities expert, and have no intention of becoming one, then spending your time thinking about your investments is only going to cost you in other areas.

While I understand why someone would want to get a better understanding of investing, there are technologies and services that exist that can take care of this for you. Do yourself a favour and focus on what you do best.

CHAPTER SUMMARY

Q *How this helps fund your ideal lifestyle?*

Your ideal lifestyle in the future will be less about taking risks and enjoying adventures and more about mitigating risk and enjoying comforts.

Figuring out what your 'comfort amount' needs are, and then calculating the asset base required to meet those ongoing needs will ensure you live an ideal lifestyle far into the future also.

Q *How to make this easy?*

Funnelling a small amount of money aside without much thought to investing in a low cost and low tax environment, will ensure you build up a large asset base to draw an income from when you no longer work, with little to no effort.

You don't want to think about investing too much as unless you become an expert you're wasting your time. Investing can be seen as sexy – and we are going to get more into it shortly, but you don't need to think about it. All you need is a low fee and low tax environment to build a diversified portfolio that doesn't need much of your ongoing attention. Focus on the things that are really important to you instead.

STE

AUTO

CASH

EP 2
MATE
FLOW

"PEOPLE DON'T WANT TO BE MILLION-AIRES, THEY WANT TO LIVE THE LIFESTYLE THEY THINK ONLY MILLIONS CAN BUY."

- TIM FERRIS, *THE FOUR HOUR WORK WEEK*

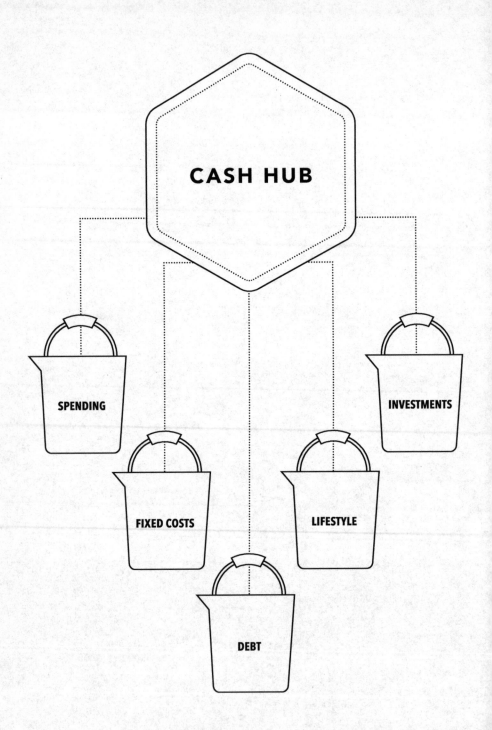

FIVE BUCKET METHOD

More money doesn't make life better, better money management does. In this section, I've laid out in detail how you can organise your cash flow so you remain in control while outsourcing the difficult decisions to technology.

I call it the Five Bucket Method and it has produced success not only for myself, but for my clients also. The aim is not to look at your regular income as one large amount, but instead as five separate amounts to help you fund each vital area of your life.

SIX

MONSTERS EAT MONEY

THE FIXED COST BUCKET

"WIN FIRST, AND THEN GO TO WAR."

- SUN TZU, *THE ART OF WAR*

"A FOOL AND HIS MONEY ARE SOON PARTED."

- THOMAS TUSSER,
FIVE HUNDRED POINTS OF GOOD HUSBANDRY

LATE TO BED, LATE TO RISE

t's 11 am on a Tuesday. I'm 20 years old, and I'm still in bed. Not that it matters. Amateur rock stars don't live by 'the rules' anyway.

I decide with regret that it's time to start my day, mostly because I'm finally unsuccessful getting back to sleep for the fifth time this morning and the room is starting to heat up from the midday sun. I can hear murmurs coming from downstairs and the distinct clinking of someone cleaning up beer bottles in the living room.

FIXED COST

I'll probably head down to the beach sometime today, followed by some intense Xbox, and maybe play a round of mini golf in the backyard course we have built by mowing fairways in the long grass and sticking tin cans in the ground.

I wander out and see we have a couple of additional guests for the night still snoozing on the beanbags. I've seen them before; I think they have something to do with the music industry so they're welcome to stay the night. Anyone is.

And today is just like any other day. Wake up just before midday, roughly clean up from the night before, get down to the beach around lunch, come back home and spend some time finalising the lyrics of the latest song we are writing (the lyrics have to make sense, but not too much sense).

Play some pool or hang in the small blow-up pool on the veranda, and wait till our drummer finishes school so we can have a two-hour practice session before some more friends turn up with beers around 9 pm. Then we'll party into the night.

Ahh yes, the life. I get noticed in music shops and asked for autographs. Girls treat me as if I'm legitimately famous (I'm not), and I'm talking with record labels and sponsors. The only problem is, and I'm well aware of it, we aren't good enough for this to last forever.

Come late-2004, our band dissolved with the promise to fans that we'd be getting back together in a year (we never did) and I was lost. All I had known was screaming into microphones, and what else was out there for a young man with too many ear piercings?

Luckily six months later, I met a young entrepreneur from Canada. His energy was infectious, and his stories were compelling as he told me all about how he makes a fortune while travelling the world and having a great time. I felt inspired and, for the first time in a long time, had a glimmer of hope of what I wanted to achieve in life again.

He told me I could use my creativity for more than writing semi-suggestive, semi-esoteric lyrics to unmemorable melody lines. Before he left, he bought me a copy of *Rich Dad Poor Dad* and left a note inside the cover to go out there and do something besides lament a failed project.

I read the book, and it was like learning a language I never knew existed. I then devoured all of Robert Kiyosaki's books and his suggested reading list.

Over the course of the next couple of months, I dedicated myself to the subject of personal finance. I built myself a calculator in an Excel spreadsheet and gave myself six months to get out of debt. It became such a passion I ended up enrolling the next year into accounting.

LEARNING THE HARD WAY

All this newfound knowledge came in handy. I was twenty-one years old, working part-time as a painter, and just started university. I also had a mountain of debt. That's right. Well before I had a degree in accounting or an office in a Sydney skyscraper, I learned about the importance of mastering cash flow because I had to grit my teeth and get through it myself.

It was here that I found out about the adverse effects of fixed costs on an overall financial outcome. Fixed costs it turns out, is the number one thing standing in the way of funding your ideal lifestyle.

Here's why. Fixed costs put your expenses out of your control. For example, if I don't want an apple, I don't purchase the apple. I'm in control. However, if I subscribe to an apple-a-day delivery service, I have to spend money on the apple even if I don't want it. I'm not in control.

A liability or fixed cost will take money from you whether you want to spend it or not. It's a monster that eats your money in the background without any regard to your financial situation. It controls your financial decision-making ability, not the other way around.

So, to put myself back in the driver's seat, I did everything I could to reduce my fixed costs. I moved into a tiny apartment, pushed as much money as possible to my debts so I wouldn't have to continue paying minimum repayments, ceased my charitable donations, and called all my product providers to give me the best deal possible.

A liability or fixed cost will take money from you whether you want to spend it or not. It's a monster that eats your money in the background without any regard to your financial situation. It controls your financial decision making ability, not the other way around.

Then I set up my spending plan, made it as strict as humanly possible on myself, and decided with the temerity of free solo climber that I was going to make this happen in record time.

Overnight, I turned into the most virtuous twenty-one-year-old monk. I spent six months without touching a single drop of alcohol or going out for a single meal. Not because I decided I needed to go on a health kick but to put all my money aside for debt. If lifestyle inflation is a common problem, I suffered an intense bout of lifestyle deflation.

After I had made the decision to stop going out, I then reduced my weekly spending on groceries to an abysmal $17.50 per week . In hindsight, I regret making the process such a burden. I've since learned it's not about going from spending too much to saving too much; it's about balance.

The bad news was I lost a few kilos, had poor nutrition, and was super bored for six months. The good news was I had a very successful university semester, and completely turned my financial situation around.

The result was great, but my method was rudimentary. I made the process far harder on myself than necessary.

So it was this trial and error in my life that fostered the skills I would later use to create a service to help others. I learned how to master cash flow not through just reading about it, but by doing it. And that is a big difference. Everything I know about money, I have lived every step.

What I learned during this financially touchy time of my life, ended up becoming the biggest insight I have into what makes someone financially successful or not. Though the sums of money on which I cut my teeth are far different from the numbers my clients have these days, the fundamentals are the same.

What I learned academically and implemented into my life, I then turned into a service to handle the financial lives of other people. To see their ongoing success mirror my own, I now have no doubt mastering your cash flow will have the biggest positive effect on achieving what you want out of life now and in the future.

And that's the purpose of this second section of the book. It's all about making the most of your money. Knowing how to get the most out of your weekly income is the most important thing you can do as everything else falls into place.

IF YOU'RE GOOD WITH CASH FLOW...

...you're probably not going to get into credit card debt.

...you're going to know how much to put aside to purchase a home.

...you're going to be able to start building an asset base for long-term wealth creation.

...you're probably going to understand more about money than most people.

...you'll be well-equipped to fund your ideal lifestyle.

Figuring out what you want out of life is always the first, and arguably the hardest step; the second is to filter out your money automatically. Mastering your cash flow takes your lifestyle aspirations and makes them a reality.

ONGOING COMFORTS

"THE LIFE WE RECEIVE IS NOT SHORT, BUT WE MAKE IT SO, NOR DO WE HAVE ANY LACK OF IT, BUT ARE WASTEFUL OF IT. JUST AS GREAT AND PRINCELY WEALTH IS SCATTERED IN A MOMENT WHEN IT COMES INTO THE HANDS OF A BAD OWNER, WHILE WEALTH HOWEVER LIMITED, IF IT IS ENTRUSTED TO A GOOD GUARDIAN, INCREASES BY USE, SO OUR LIFE IS AMPLY LONG FOR HIM WHO ORDERS IT PROPERLY."

- LUCIUS ANNAEUS SENECA, *ON THE SHORTNESS OF LIFE*

You could survive in the Amazon jungle for $5 a day, including accommodation and food, and yet most people will happily pay that for a membership they don't even use.

If you earn a decent living, it's easy to assume you also take it for granted. But here is the kicker. It's not so much what you earn, or how you spend your money on shoes, dinners, or weekend flights. The main cause of financial trouble: fixed costs.

Fixed costs are the elephant in the room that no one wants to talk about. People sacrifice their life for a higher income, but rarely do anything to reduce their ongoing financial commitments.

Fixed costs are not expenses. Expenses are fun. You get an emotional reward from the excitement of jumping on the plane to this year's bucket list destination or buying a new shirt. But who gets excited about receiving a phone bill in the mail?

Reducing ongoing fixed costs is the best thing you can do to get more money in your pocket. You do it once, and every week the potential for you to do more with your money goes up.

So instead of racking up unending subscriptions that cost you money every day without your knowledge, let's talk about what else you could do with that money besides nonchalantly waste it.

Let's find you some new experiences.

What we want to do is give you a way to spend your money so you enjoy it, rather than have it just disappear. And as humans, we will always spend the amount we allocate to ourselves.

If we reduce the amount of money you are willing to put aside for fixed costs every week, you have more money to use as you choose. The power shifts from external to internal; your financial decisions are not being dictated to you. Instead, they answer to your free will.

And so to have control over your money, we start with reducing your fixed costs. The amount that goes up in smoke the moment you wake up in the morning and roll out of bed.

So what does that mean? We're talking about rental amounts or mortgage payments, gym membership, minimum credit card or personal loan repayments, insurances, phone bills or any other bills that are regular.

·············· **EXERCISE 6.1** ··············

Write a list of all the financial commitments you have, what they cost, and the frequency you are charged.

FIXED COST	FREQUENCY	AMOUNT
FIXED COST	FREQUENCY	AMOUNT
FIXED COST	FREQUENCY	AMOUNT
FIXED COST	FREQUENCY	AMOUNT
FIXED COST	FREQUENCY	AMOUNT
FIXED COST	FREQUENCY	AMOUNT

QUANTIFYING THE MONSTER

Now that you have your list, break these amounts down to a weekly average. Regardless of how frequently each cost occurs, if you create a weekly standard for all income and outgoings, it is far easier to make this work[34].

Because fixed costs need to be paid regardless of whether you want to or not, it's not your money. You have no control over these funds, it simply glides from you to the employer's bank account to the fixed cost, passing through your bank account only for the scenic tour.

As such, the best description for your weekly fixed costs is a reduction in your salary. And any new and regular fixed cost you take on is accepting a further drop in salary.

Used well these fixed costs help pay for things that genuinely make your life better. However, most of the time this is not the case. Most of the time fixed costs are the biggest cause of most financial unravelling. Let me explain.

Fixed costs are there to help you enjoy your life. Do you like to live in nice apartments close to your favourite beach and cafes? Well, there is going to be a high price for that. Namely, because everyone else feels the same way.

Do you like your clean and new gym? Well, that is going to cost you. What about your new car, your private membership to the racetrack, your ongoing wine delivery? All of these will either add to your lifestyle or take away from it.

Now I have no doubt when you first signed up for whatever it is that tickled your fancy at that time was a good idea. It doesn't matter. The only thing I care about is when your interest wanes

34 / Go to www.fundyourideallifestyle.com.au/calculator for an easier way to calculate.

and your usage drops, don't just keep the ongoing fixed cost. Cancel it.

Too many times I've seen a new fixed cost, which initially brought joy to someone's life, slowly become unused. But the fact that the app or service or subscription is getting ignored doesn't change the price. The fixed costs stay the same. This is what I call 'lifestyle inflation'.

We just accept this ongoing reduction in our income is what it costs to live the way we enjoy our life, and then we sign up to the next one. We take out car loans and personal loans, rack up credit card debt – all of which require more and more ongoing repayments. And each fixed cost you take on stacks on the last, and the monster gets bigger and bigger and eats more of your money each week.

And now the monster is happy. He just sits there, all giant. Imposing his will on you, spending your money before you even get the chance.

That's why the first thing I always do with a new client is figure out their ongoing fixed costs before anything else. I want to see what someone's *real* income is before we start filtering it out.

This one step has potentially the biggest impact of all. When someone walks into my office and tells me they make $200,000 per year, the first thing I do is figure out their weekly income less tax, and less their ongoing liabilities. When they see for the first time the amount of money they have control over, it's often a very sobering moment.

OPTIMAL BREAKDOWN

The first rule of keeping more of what you've worked for is to know how much is being taken from your income in fixed costs before you get to spend it. The second is keeping in mind some general rules of thumb.

I created these rules of thumb from tracking my most successful clients for twelve months after we worked together. Filtering your money out as follows will ensure you keep your fixed costs down, while at the same time allowing a good amount to be spent guilt-free, and making sure tomorrow is looked after as well.

The breakdown of the pie graph below represents the average spend per bucket by my most successful clients. Fixed costs make up the majority of the spend at 40%; weekly spending money received around 30%, and debt, lifestyle, and investing all received an equal 10%.

IDEAL BUDGET

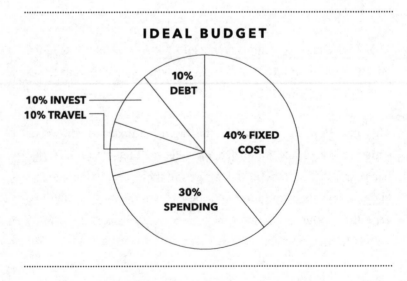

IDEAL SPENDING PLAN

For those who don't have any debt or pay it down, the 10% allocated to debt can be split evenly between the lifestyle bucket and the investment bucket resulting in 15% for each.

Others who have substantial debt can put a hold on the lifestyle bucket and the investment bucket for twelve months and direct 30% towards debt. If a good dent has been made into the debt owing, introducing the lifestyle and investment bucket can be done then.

The main takeaway was that the fixed cost monster was limited to under 50% of total income including housing (rent or mortgage), gym, phone, car, and all other ongoing fixed costs.

With all this in mind, it's not hard to understand that the higher your fixed costs, the less likely you are to achieve a good outcome. As they take up the biggest piece of the pie, fixed costs are the main culprits in lifestyle inflation.

If your fixed costs rise at the same pace as your pay rises, you haven't actually received a pay rise at all. If your salary reduction simply meets your pay increase, then the amount of money you have control over has not increased at all.

The first time I met a client earning above $200,000 per year and in $100,000 credit card debt, I couldn't believe it. When I looked deeper into the situation, I immediately found the issue. Fixed costs, including housing, were above 90%.

This person was so convinced their salary could provide an unquestionable lifestyle they never thought to do anything about the excessive amount of money haemorrhaging from their back pockets in fixed costs before they even had the chance to spend any themselves.

We cut his bloated fixed costs with ferocity and redirected his surplus cash to pay down his debt. After twelve months of hard work, we were still able to get him overseas without more debt.

But the biggest improvement we made was reducing his fixed costs. There would have been no chance for success unless we had approached his current fixed costs with the intention to reduce them drastically. These ongoing liabilities had the biggest effect on his day-to-day income, and by taking care of that issue, we were able to get him back from the brink of bankruptcy.

Going over your fixed costs to ensure you aren't leaking money has a hidden additional advantage. Any change you make to reduce your fixed costs benefits you every day. In the same way, they can be a monster eating away your money in the background, any reduction you make in your ongoing liabilities will be beneficial to you, day in day out, without you having to work for it. Your fixed costs go down, the amount of money you have in your control goes up again, and you essentially receive a pay rise.

I always look for the easiest way to accomplish things, and with spending, it's best to win first, before you even begin. By that, I mean spend the time to take care of something that will leverage your efforts. Identifying and reducing your fixed costs is in no small way the most effective thing you can do to have more money to help fund your ideal lifestyle.

CHAPTER SUMMARY

....

Q *How this helps fund your ideal lifestyle?*

Reducing your fixed costs gives you more control of your own money to spend on things that are important to you. The less money you have tied up in financial commitments, the less stress you have to bring in that amount every week.

If you are looking for new employment options, the fewer financial obligations you have, the more likely you are to take the risk of trying something new. The people I have seen start new careers, move cities, or even ask for promotions were under less pressure to bring in the weekly paycheque – and that is achieved by reducing fixed costs.

Q *How to make this easy?*

Turning down something you want to do just to save your money is hard. And every time you want to spend it, you have to make that decision. However, as fixed costs eat your money without you thinking about it, any work you do to minimise the monster's appetite will directly translate into more money for you without extra ongoing work.

Therefore once you have discovered what your ongoing financial commitments are, do research to reduce them. The most impactful change is in housing. Is it a lot of work to change your living situation? Yes, but if you are spending a ridiculous amount on rent or mortgage, then this should be an option.

But there are many smaller things you can do easily. Electricity companies, for example will give discounts straight away. Call your utility company and say if you don't get an ongoing discount you'll leave. Do it with every service provider you use. Demand a lower interest rate on your credit card if you have credit card debt. Get creative and email me your results! I love hearing about unique ways people have reduced their fixed costs.

Now, on to the How-To. Once you have reduced your fixed costs as much as possible, call each company and redirect all payments to a separate account. You want to avoid having all your incomings and outgoings from the one account as it's impossible to track everything.

Bank account statements are not built for consumers; they are built for banks. By directing all fixed costs to a separate account, all you have to do is ensure enough money per week is in the account. You won't have to think of your fixed costs again until you either add or remove more.

SEVEN

DOPAMINE SPIKES

THE SPENDING BUCKET

"I LOVE MONEY. I LOVE EVERYTHING ABOUT IT.

I BOUGHT SOME PRETTY GOOD STUFF.

GOT ME A $300 PAIR OF SOCKS.

GOT A FUR SINK. AN ELECTRIC DOG POLISHER.

A GASOLINE POWERED TURTLENECK SWEATER.

AND, OF COURSE, I BOUGHT SOME DUMB STUFF, TOO."

- STEVE MARTIN

"I SPENT A LOT OF MONEY ON BOOZE, BIRDS, AND FAST

CARS. THE REST I JUST SQUANDERED."

- GEORGE BEST

'm walking along a beach in some shorts, a singlet, and a pair of thongs. It's nearly midnight, and I'm out with some of my best friends. Also joining us in this intimate setting are ten thousand other people, loud dance music, alcohol in buckets[35], flames, and fireworks.

It's New Year's Eve 2009/10 and I'm in the Ibiza of Asia, the island of Koh Phangan off the coast of Thailand. And as the dark expanse of the universe subsides to the morning shades of blue and yellow, with waves lapping against my ankles I realise I like this travel thing.

After arriving home from Thailand, I worked for another six months and took off again to Eastern Europe. This time, I jumped on a bicycle and rode from Prague, down to Vienna, across to Bratislava and then down into Budapest.

The fact that I had not ridden a bike since high school was irrelevant. I now had money coming in from full-time work, so the question ceased to be 'how' I could afford something, but rather became 'when' do I want to do it?

My dad had ridden around the UK when he was younger, and in amongst all his travel experiences told me it was right at the top. Not willing to be outdone by my old man, I saddled up and stayed upright for a full month[36] as I travelled through four countries.

When I returned back to Australia and back to work, I knew it

35 / Buckets I feel, should be a legitimate unit of measure for alcohol.

36 / Though only just. At one point I was speeding down a hill and hit a pothole. I came up over the handlebars to the point I was balancing on just the front wheel and the other wheel swang around to my righthand side until I could see it. Thankfully I was able to gain control again and keep going.

was useless to fight the travel bug I so clearly had. I saw out the rest of the year, said goodbye to my tax accounting career, and took off to South America with a one-way ticket.

MORE THAN DOLLAR SIGNS

Spending money is fun. It really is. And having listened to people talk about money for the last decade I have no reason to question anyone feels differently. Money is transportable power; it allows people to do what they want when they want. And the more money you have to spend, the more you can afford to do, and the more fun you can have.

As such, the topic of money is emotional. Even for me. I don't give financial advice to family members as I'm too connected, and I filter my income through the Five Bucket method.

And that's normal. That's natural. It's impossible to look at your income with no regard to your future. Your immediate and future plans all depend on your money situation. And it's the management of your money rather than how much you make which has the biggest impact on reaching those plans.

When I left for South America, it wasn't a high salary affording me the ability to make that decision. At the time I was in a graduate position and making only $45,000. My advantage, however, was I had put every salary through a calculator since I was twenty-one.

Being emotionally attached to your income means it is almost impossible to make the right decisions with it. And even if you're some kind of cyborg and able to do so, the amount of decision fatigue you waste on those decisions each week does not warrant you making these decisions in the first place.

That's why the whole premise of the Five Bucket method is to create cognitive minimalism. Remove your fallible self from making decisions around your income each week because a) you're too emotionally involved to make the best decisions, and b) by making these decisions, you reduce the quality of your choices in every area of your life.

And while redirecting a portion of your salary to an account that then pays for all your fixed costs is one thing, redirecting the second portion for you to spend each week guilt-free is another one entirely. That is exactly what I'm proposing.

Often when people are paid monthly, they go out and start spending. This makes sense as their available cash goes from 'broke' to 'plenty'. I'll make this clear: you will spend according to how much is in your account. If there is a lot in your account, you will feel justified to spend a lot.

Fortnightly payment has a similar effect, though not as extreme. And weekly payment, while avoiding that particular mess, creates its own set of chaotic problems. Therefore, regardless of how often your salary is paid, this money should be paid to a cash hub you can't access easily. Then the cash hub moves an amount to your spending bucket on a regular basis. Best of all, it happens in the background without you having to think about it.

This creates space for cognitive minimalism by avoiding the

need to make any decisions about a highly emotional topic – your money[37].

This Five Bucket method is about removing you, the imperfect, emotionally invested, faulty person who is currently taking care of your finances, and putting a predetermined system in your place. One that is perfect, one that doesn't have emotions, and one that holds you accountable even when you don't want to be.

One day a young guy in his late twenties walked into my office with an air of dishevelled determination. His long hair flowed down his face, losing itself in his beard like a team of rivers tangling in an ocean. He earned good money, though he had nothing to show for it. He didn't need a higher salary; he needed better money management.

We organised a daily payment arrangement. He went from receiving his fortnightly pay and handling every financial decision himself to the Five Bucket method, where his only relationship to his money was a daily amount that turned up in his bank account.

All it took was outsourcing his financial decisions, and in a year he went from being in debt to putting aside 10% of his wage towards a deposit for his first property.

Because spending money is fun, you have to put aside an amount of money each week to go crazy with, to waste however you like. On lunch? On a date? On a weekend getaway? Spend this money however you choose.

---

37 / If you still struggle with weekly amounts, my pro tip is to pay yourself twice: once on Friday and once on Monday. Most overspending I have found happens on the weekend, so by having an amount waiting for you on Monday, it reduces your ability to overspend during the weekend.

If you want to step it up a notch and get really serious, what you can do is take all the cash you plan on spending for the week and put it in your wallet or purse for the week ahead.

Using cash has an extra layer of effectiveness as we have an inbuilt system, created from when we were very young, not to spend paper money. Let me explain. When you were a child and couldn't earn much outside of pocket money, Christmas's and birthdays were the only way you could get some cash together.

Because we learned how hard money was to come by when we were young, we have kept a small amount of resistance to simply handing it over. Our initial relationship to hard cash in the hand was one of scarcity. Sure, that may not be the case now, but at least you have some measure of inbuilt self-control.

Compare that to using a card. Credit or debit – it doesn't matter – when it comes to plastic, we have zero inbuilt resistance. No part of our upbringing prepared us for tapping a card on a machine. It's so easy and simple; it's as if you aren't spending the money in the first place.

Which is why using cash instead of a card is another pro tip to help you achieve the goal of allocating your money and spending it guilt-free each week. Not only do you have the inbuilt resistance, watching the number of notes in your wallet decline gives you a visual cue to know where you are for the rest of the week.

DIMISHING RETURNS OF MONEY

Whether you are a natural saver or spender, moving to a situation where you are perfectly balanced will give you the greatest benefit.

Once you know how much your fixed costs and weekly spending money come to, you'll know exactly how much it costs for you to live the life to which you have grown accustomed.

In Chapter Four you completed an exercise to figure out what you would like to be able to afford each week. Every day, as you get out of bed and go about your business, think about this: What are the things you want to have in your life?

That's where your spending money comes in. Fixed costs take care of financial responsibilities but offer nothing by way of spikes in your dopamine, but your spending money is used to fund your ideal lifestyle today. Whether it's a new shirt, new shoes, or going out to dinner, this money is there for you to have a good time with it.

Knowing upfront how much you have available to spend just on yourself on a weekly basis reduces decision fatigue and promotes cognitive minimalism by reducing your purchasing options. This type of positive restraint also ensures you don't suffer from the consequences of overspending.

Epicurus said finding balance in your spending and avoiding insatiability keeps you in control. I can't put enough emphasis on the effects of overspending. Not only does it ruin your ideal lifestyle in the future whether by reducing the amount to spend on your next holiday, or lessening the amount of income you can receive when you no longer work, but it is the biggest enemy of cognitive minimalism.

Overspending causes stress, guilt, associated health problems, but worse of all it becomes the screen saver to your mind. Overspending causes you to make many more decisions, juggling your financial situation until you get back on top. Put simply: overspending is no longer guilt-free spending.

Directly receiving a predictable and ongoing salary is the all contributing factor in this type of overspending lifestyle. The basic thought behind it is, 'Why bother spending less when I know I have more money coming in next pay day?'

Some people manage to handle their money coming in each week, but self-discipline is a lousy way to get things done. Even if you don't suffer from overspending, why manage your money directly, and be forced to decide what to do with it and where it goes, when you can have it all set up on automated direct debits by your bank?

But this doesn't have to happen. If you know where your money is going with your buckets,[38] your increased awareness will engage you more with the outcome.

Once you have spent some time figuring out much is being spent on fixed costs, and how much you can reasonably afford to send yourself each week, your guilt-free spending money becomes exactly that, guilt-free.

Overspending is also a symptom of overworking. With so much stress, often the most common way of 'cooling off' is to spend money. However, this creates an income trap. Once addicted to high spending, your dependence on your income also rises. This is called lifestyle inflation, and it's a nasty cycle.

Instead, when you move from overspending to spending a predetermined amount, you avoid lifestyle inflation, improve your

38 / Go to www.fundyourideallifestyle.com.au/calculator

financial situation, and benefit from cognitive minimalism by reduced stress and improved performance at work.

MINDLESS MONEY

We have on average two hundred thoughts about what to eat each
day[39] from something as small as buying a coffee, to whether we
will go out for dinner with friend's tomorrow night. Each of these
involves a purchasing decision.

Add to this the amount of direct financial thoughts we have each
day and the knowledge we are coming up against billions of
dollars' worth of research into how to distract you with advertising, and you start to realise how hard it is for us to succeed
without a plan.

If you have no plan to tackle these thoughts, no greater idea beyond 'I want this, how will I pay for it?' you will succumb to
these impulses as your ability to make smart decisions each day
gets worn away with decision fatigue.

On the other hand giving yourself a regular amount of spending
money gives you the freedom to know exactly how much you can
spend guilt-free each week without it having an impact on your
long-term plans.

For example, let's say you pay yourself $500 on Monday and
use $100 through the week on lunch and bits and pieces. You
have dinner with friends Friday night and lunch on Sunday, cost-
ing you another $100 for the whole weekend. Even though you

---

39 / 'Mindless Eating The 200 Daily Food Decisions We Overlook' Wansink, B., Sobal, S.

know you can spend that additional $300 you don't. Because guess what? Next weekend you're off to Melbourne and want to pay for flights.

Separating your money down to the smallest amount possible makes it infinitely easier to predict, to plan, and to stick to your strategy. When you have industries devoted to separating you from your money, walking out the front door with a plan significantly increases your chance at success.

It's not about tracking every cent, finding out where you're spending the most and 'cutting down on spending'. It's being aware that without a plan, you're up against a well-co-ordinated attack to get you to overspend your money.

Knowing upfront how much you can happily spend every week removes you from the centre of your financial life and allows you to ensure your travel plans in six months are looking good, as is your long term wealth creation strategies to pay you an income in the future when you no longer work.

CHAPTER SUMMARY

Q *How this helps fund your ideal lifestyle?*

Knowing how much money you have to spend each week allows you to fund your ideal lifestyle today. By allocating yourself a predictable amount that fits in with your overall plan, you drastically reduce the chances of overspending.

It also removes you from decision fatigue. If you have access to your entire salary at your fingertips, then everything and anything is a potential purchase for you. This results in reduced cognitive minimalism and lower quality performance in every area of your life.

Q *How to make this easy?*

Have your employment or business income deposited into a separate cash hub. Then organise automatic weekly payments to an account you do control. If weekly doesn't work well, try once on Friday and once on Monday. Avoid overspending and all the associated problems by using this amount to enjoy your life today.

PAYING TWICE

THE DEBT BUCKET

"I'M LIVING SO FAR BEYOND MY INCOME,
THAT WE MAY ALMOST BE SAID TO BE LIVING APART."

- E.E. CUMMINGS

"ANNUAL INCOME TWENTY POUNDS, ANNUAL EXPENDITURE
NINETEEN SIX, RESULT HAPPINESS.
ANNUAL INCOME TWENTY POUNDS, ANNUAL EXPENDITURE
TWENTY POUND AND SIX, RESULT MISERY."

- CHARLES DICKENS, DAVID COPPERFIELD

FROM BEHIND THE STARTING BLOCKS

With pupils dilated, and a bead of sweat falling down your brow, you walk out of a locker room and meet the ushers who lead you to a door. You've been training for this moment for the last ten years, but now you are here, you don't have time to consider the magnitude of what's about to happen.

You have your earphones in, listening to the same pre-race track list you've been listening to for the last three competitions. You've won each of your last three races, so you're not going to change it now.

A light above the door turns from red to green; it's time for business. You open the door and start your walk to the light at the end of the tunnel. Out there, you know it's pandemonium.

As you step out from the cold cement room behind you, you look up at the sky. It's a bright day today, and your eyes take a second to adjust. Then you see the size of the crowd. Eighty thousand people have crammed into the stadium, and millions more are watching at home, all waiting for you to run one hundred meters faster than anyone has in history.

As you take it all in, you start the long walk down the track. Your competitors are all here now, warming up, jumping, stretching. They're as prepared as you are, and in five short minutes, the world will remember why you're the champ.

There's only one problem. As you get to the starting line, you notice all the blocks are set up correctly, except yours. While the other lanes have the blocks positioned correctly, yours are positioned ten meters back from everyone else.

Livid, you turn to the officials and complain, but as they explain, this is your correct starting position. Behind everyone else. It will waste precious time just to make up the deficit. While the rest of the field will be speeding ahead, you will be making up lost ground, just trying to get to the starting line.

This frustrating setback is what it's like to have debt. While everyone else around you is charging ahead and building momentum, you're working furiously to catch up, wasting precious time before you can even start your race.

The hidden menace of holding debt is that it restricts your ability to get ahead of it. This often-overlooked fact should be at the forefront of your mind when determining how to deal with your existing debt or whether to take on new debt.

For example, if you have thirty thousand dollars in credit card debt, you have a two-fold problem. Firstly, due to interest rates, you're going to pay much more than what you originally paid. Secondly, it's an anchor around your neck, stopping you from gaining forward momentum.

Building up a war chest of money is important as it allows you to purchase assets to fund your ideal lifestyle when you no longer work. However before you can start, you need to pay off debt first. The reason is, there's a good chance the interest payable on the debt will be greater than the interest rate received by the assets. In other words, more money will be going out than coming in. Therefore, it's pointless to start building assets until the majority of your debt is paid off.

This point deserves your attention since the earlier you start building assets, the better. And the quicker you pay off debt, the quicker you can start to build assets with the money that you're currently committing to ongoing debt repayments. How much better is that? Instead of giving your money to the bank, you are building an asset base for yourself.

Remember, fixed costs are a reduction in income. If the minimum repayments on your debt are a thousand dollars a month, and you pay off the debt, your income is no longer reduced by a thousand dollars per month. It's the equivalent of getting a $1,000 a month pay rise.

THE GOOD, THE BAD AND THE UNSAFE

All debt was considered a bad thing in my family. I say that, with full knowledge of where that comment places my family on the wealth spectrum. From experience, it's usually those with the least amount of money who like to espouse such truths.

I say this because although my parents didn't know much about debt and avoided all of it, I've noticed most people don't really understand debt either. At best I may hear about a very rudimentary judgment on debt as either 'good debt[40]', or 'bad debt[41]'.

However, even good debt has levels of safety. If the asset earns you money each week, then it is safe to hold. Your fixed costs

40 / Good debt is considered to be any debt taken on to fund the purchase of assets that go up in value. A home mortgage would be a example.

41 / Bad debt is any debt connected to anything that is not an asset expected to increase in value. Purchasing a car with a loan would be a common example.

don't go up, and you can repay the loan regardless of whether you move to a new country, change jobs, or take an extended vacation. There will never be a situation where you are ever pressured to sell.

If the asset does cost you money each week, then it is unsafe to hold. This good debt depends on your ability to pay it back. Your fixed costs increase, and the amount of money you have control over decreases.

The big mistake I see most people make is to think all assets purchased with good debt automatically means a sound investment decision. That is false. If you bought an asset with debt and it costs you money on a regular basis, this may be good debt, but it isn't very safe.

The safety of debt depends on how easy it is to keep up with the repayments, and whether the only chance to make money is by taking on the risk of the asset price going up over time. If you are out of pocket each week due to expenses and relying on the asset to increase in value over time to make a profit, you may have taken on good debt that is also 'unsafe'.

Safe debt, as you can imagine, is harder to find, but far from impossible. For example, when I started my financial advice company I purchased a small professional services business which paid a higher rate of return than what it cost me to hold the debt.

As the debt was used to purchase an asset expected to grow in value, we can call it good debt. And since the income received from the asset was greater than the cost to borrow the money, the debt was also safe.

Access to this debt was an important part of my business growth in the early stages and was pivotal in my early success. As such, I am very well aware of the power of good debt. In order to ensure the debt is also safe, you should be most concerned with the quality of the investment you purchase. Debt is a very powerful tool. Which way you leverage is the question.

NOT ALL DEBT IS CREATED EQUAL

While the difference between good and bad debt is easy to identify, let's go through some exercises to examine whether the debt is safe or not.

EXERCISE 8.1

Which of the following is good debt with an interest rate of 5%?

- $5,000 spent on clothes with a credit card.

- $500,000 investment property paying 8% income.

- $5,000,000 investment property paying 3% income.

- $50,000,000 to build a product producing 50% income.

I'd comfortably say the vast majority of people would look at the first option and have a lot of reluctance to say it is good debt as it is credit card debt. Of course, there are those legendary stories of companies like Atlassian bootstrapping themselves with $10,000 on a credit card, but as we can see here this is just consumer debt.

So $5,000 spent on clothes with a credit card is bad debt.

The second one is a little easier. We have purchased an investment property for $500,000 with debt, and it is paying 8% income. Because the interest rate on the loan is only 5%, we have the remaining 3% to handle repairs and maintenance, council rates, rental management and strata fees, with the rest going towards paying down the original loan. Because we are not out of pocket every week while holding the asset, it is good and safe debt.

Then we come to our third option. We've borrowed $5,000,000 to buy an investment property, but it's only paying 3%, which doesn't even cover the ongoing 5% interest charge, let alone all the other ongoing costs. It will cost us money to hold, and while the property will undoubtedly go up in value over time (making it 'good' debt), because the investment costs us money every week, it is good debt, but not considered safe.

The final option is an interesting one as we are now part of a venture capital buy-in. The company had achieved its early goals and now selling $50,000,000 in equity to finish funding. Once the expansion is complete in twelve months, this will pay 50% per year in dividends. While the asset being purchased is no longer a retail investment[42] and becomes a whole lot more complex, this is an example of good debt that is safe as the investment pays for itself[43].

The point is, there are many investments sold on the benefits of

42 / Retail investments are simple investments available to everyone. The most profitable investments are of course the most risky and are only available to 'sophisticated investors'.

43 / While the debt is good and safe, the likelihood of start-ups failing means the investment itself is not particularly safe. We will go in to more detail in chapter 14.

using 'good debt', but that is not a real measure of success. Anyone can get into debt. What you really want is for the debt to be 'safe' also. There are countless salespeople willing to take your money and sell you assets that cost you money on a weekly basis to hold.

Examine each investment on a case-by-case scenario. I wish all investments purchased with good debt could be considered a great investment, but that simply isn't so.

MINIMUM REPAYMENTS

One of the most infuriating parts of the money hijinks played out by the big institutions is the concept of minimum repayments on credit card debt. I'm not entirely sure why this is even legal. It's not hard to see they are designed to keep people in debt as long as possible.

As you've probably picked up over the course of this book, delaying your ability to start moving ahead in life, growing assets, and building a future does not benefit you in any way.

Being in debt for longer extends the distance you have to make up in your 100m sprint. It increases your fixed costs thereby reducing the amount of your money you control, and you end up paying much more than what you originally paid. All of these are horrible, and minimum repayments only extend the life of this problem.

The companies that issue the debt, on the other hand, love minimum repayments. Interest is hands down the easiest way for them to make money. So imagine what they think about charging interest on your consumer debt of 20% per year? They love it! The longer you're in debt, the more they benefit. Don't just pay the minimum repayments. Pay your debt down aggressively.

FROM REVERSE TO FAST FORWARD

Having seen scores of people walk through my door with some debt, and then walk out after a few months with no debt and the first savings they have ever had, I'd like to share their results with you.

Simone walked into my office with some credit card debt, a penchant for overspending, and a drawer full of unpaid road tolls. All in all, she had around $20,000 in unpaid bills and credit card debt.

She worked in finance, was on a decent wage, and no one ever would have thought her to be anything but on top of her game. However, she was weighed down by her debt. It was a constant distraction, and her potential was diminished due to the fact there was this huge number sitting on the sidelines waiting for her.

Realising this debt needed to be taken care of quickly, we redirected all spare cash using automated transfers to the debt for a couple of months, and when her bonus came in we were able to take care of the rest.

This approach was only possible because she knew exactly where her bonus money needed to go. If she didn't know what needed her attention, she absolutely would have gone out and spent that money just like every other time. All it took was assessing the outcomes of continuously holding debt, and she was more than willing to put together a strategy to dig herself out.

Stanford University is, of course, world-renowned for its research studies[44], and there is a famous one titled the 'Stanford Marshmallow Experiment' in which a child was given two options. The first option allowed the child to have a marshmallow immediately, or if the child could delay their satisfaction, they were allowed two marshmallows.

The study continued to follow up with these same children for the next few decades, and they found those with the ability to delay gratification had better health, better jobs, and more life fulfilment[45].

The basic lesson here is self-control improves your life, but self-control is only easy to achieve if you are aware of the consequences specific to your situation. If you're aware of problems, they are easier to remedy. The chances of someone giving up smoking because the general rule says "smoking is bad for you" is low, however, if his doctor looks him in the eye and says, 'You have six months to live if you don't quit', then the patient is likely to have greater buy-in.

Over the course of twelve months, Simone went from a young woman distracted from her potential by her financial situation to an award-winning professional at the top of her field. Once we solved the problem of her debt, she had more freedom, which in turn gave her more leverage. How much bargaining power did she have once she was winning industry awards? How much

44 / Think Stanford Prison Experiment. That's some crazy stuff right there.

45 / *Predicting Adolescent Cognitive and Self-Regulatory Competencies From Preschool Delay of Gratification: Identifying Diagnostic Conditions* (1990) Shoda, Y., Mischel, W., Peake.

more time did she have to find new experiences? How much more control do you think she had over her future?

She was afforded more autonomy, more opportunity, and got promoted in her company. She was seen as an important person in her industry even though she was younger than everyone else. More importantly, she was no longer under pressure to keep her high salary coming in to pay for debt, freeing up her headspace to make the best decisions for herself moving forward.

KILL DEBT LIVE LONGER

So let's go about reducing debt, and all the issues attached to it. Depending on how much debt you have, you are either going to want to make this your top priority or an equal priority along with your Lifestyle Bucket and Investment Bucket.

As a general rule of thumb, if your debt is greater than 10% of your annual salary, it needs to be a top priority. Debt, in this case, refers to 'bad debt'. You don't need to include mortgages here.

If your bad debt is over 10% of your annual salary, you should focus on paying this down as fast as possible. Once you get your debt under 10% of your annual salary, then you can concentrate on putting money aside for travel or other lifestyle choices while still paying down the final debt amount.

Sorting out your financial life using the Five Bucket Method helps not only monetarily, but also gives you a way to handle modern day life. And debt has the biggest adverse effect since you carry it with you wherever you go. Even if it only exists on the peripheral of your brain, it is there, waiting for you to attend to it. Constantly sitting there, interrupting you, distracting you, causing you stress and decision fatigue.

Ongoing debt pressure creates stress, which keeps your performance down and reduces your potential in all areas of your life. It then bleeds into other aspects such as relationship or health issues.

In this entire book, I would say the most crucial step to start moving in the right direction to fund your ideal lifestyle is first to take care of your debt. It's where I started many years ago, and where I've had most success handling the financial life of others.

The only problem is, it's boring. Who wants to pay for something now when it was enjoyed some time in the past? It's not the most exciting conversation at your local bar, is it? That is why you set up the automatic repayments to take care of it. If all you're focused on is the Spending Bucket on a weekly basis, and the Lifestyle Bucket from time to time (next chapter), then your debt will aggressively pay itself off in the background without you having to pay attention.

If however your total consumer debt is less than 10%, then managing it while balancing your other priorities such as travel and long-term asset accumulation becomes the priority. At low levels of debt, it is easy enough to take care of it while still building the other buckets.

CHAPTER SUMMARY

....

Q *How this helps fund your ideal lifestyle?*

Getting rid of debt as soon as possible means your income goes up as the fixed costs of regular minimum repayments go down. By getting rid of debt, you decrease the amount of money you have no control over and increase the sum you can use for yourself.

Taking down your debt also frees up your mind in a couple of ways. Financial stress won't interrupt your thought patterns during the day, which increases your effectiveness at work and removes some of the worst effects of decision fatigue.

And once the incessant pressure and stress of ongoing debt cease, an individual's potential gets released, giving them better results at work which in turn ends up with more time, more autonomy and more freedom of choice. I have seen it happen time and time again.

Q *How to make this easy?*

Using the calculator at www.fundyourideallifestyle.com.au/calculator, calculate how much you can set aside to pay down your debt aggressively. I'm not talking about your minimum repayments, which are already a part of your fixed costs. I want to know how much you can pay *on top of the minimum*. This amount is to ensure your debt is paid down as fast as possible while you still live a comfortable lifestyle.

Set up automatic payments from the cash hub (your salary account) to pay towards your debt. There will never come a day when you are happy to put your money aside to pay for something you've already enjoyed, but once you have determined your spending plan and know how much you can set aside each week, set it up in automatic payments so it happens without too much ongoing thought.

NINE

REWARDS AND OTHER CARROTS

THE LIFESTYLE BUCKET

"THE WORLD IS A BOOK AND THOSE WHO DO
NOT TRAVEL READ ONLY ONE PAGE."

- AUGUSTINE OF HIPPO

"THERE IS NOTHING THE BUSY MAN IS
LESS BUSIED WITH THAN LIVING".

- SENECA

n the case of a carrot versus a stick, I've always sided with the carrot. And the easiest way I've found to create buy-in from clients on an ongoing basis is to create a reward for all their hard work.

If I'm paying my bills, spending an appropriate amount week to week, paying down debt, and building long-term assets, I want something to look forward to. Something to hope for. Something to make putting all the effort in to sort out my financial life worthwhile.

Personally, I love spending a month in a single place in the world at any given time. After a month you have a routine, you get to know people, you have favourite cafés, places, venues, bars, restaurants, galleries, parks, and all the things that make a place real. You move beyond the surface tourist attractions and get to the heart of the place.

It isn't watching the tango in Buenos Aires that makes it unbelievable. It's the social interaction and party vibe of free champagne and hors d'oeuvres while waiting in line to get into La Cabrera[46].

It isn't the beaches of the French Riviera that makes it seem like you're in a fairytale, it's getting lost in the back streets at night after a few drinks while trying not to trip over the cobblestones.

And it's not chasing the Northern Lights that makes Finland so special; it's sweating in a small fire heated sauna locked away in the forests, before jumping into an avanto[47]. I love staying long enough to understand a place before I move on, rather than a

---

46 / If you enjoy red meat and red wine, you will love this place. My favourite restaurant in the world. lacabrera.com.ar

47 / A frozen lake, normally straight after sauna.

whirlwind tour of a few cities at once. That's my carrot. That's what I work towards.

REWARD YOURSELF

When you are young, it's easy to live in the now. Life is all about finding new experiences and exploring what the world has to offer. As you get older and planning for the future takes over, these new experiences slow down, then eventually die off.

So why does this happen? Why is it that we all simply agree to become a passive bystander in our lives, watching the classical antiquated lifestyle plan rollout in front of our very eyes? I've never understood this about humanity.

If you feel the same way, the good news we have now arrived at what I consider the reward chapter. You've done the nearly impossible by clarifying what you want out of life, you've done the hard yards of making sure your fixed costs get paid for, your debt is being reduced, and you've given yourself some boundaries as to how much you spend each week. Now let's start focusing on some bigger things you value.

To buy into this process, let's start with naming this bucket after exactly what you plan to use the money to do. What is your ideal annual purchase? That will be the name of this bucket. The generic name is 'The Lifestyle Bucket', and by personalising it, you are far less likely to dip into this account at will.

You might be willing to use $500 on a weekend away if you have 'short-term savings', but I guarantee when you get the urge to take money out of your 'Tahiti Bucket', all of a sudden you'll become far more accountable to yourself.

This bucket's purpose is easily the most fun and highly motivating, but it's also paradoxically the most difficult to see as valuable. Do you know why? Because most people are so used to simply putting anything they need on a credit card, that they struggle to see the point of diverting their money in yet another direction.

However, you're far less likely to dip into your 'Croatia Bucket' to cover overspending from a crazy weekend if you know it will have a direct effect on your upcoming Mediterranean sailing adventure. And if you feel like splashing out a thousand dollars on a new piece of clothing, pulling money from your 'Home Deposit Bucket' will probably make you think twice.

Personally, it's my favourite part of the job, as it's where you get to reward yourself for all the hard work you've done to get here. And if you've been implementing these strategies as you've been reading, you'll know you deserve to treat yourself. Think about it:

- You've done what most people never do: spent the awkward and uncomfortable time to make a decision on your purpose in life.

- Taken your purpose and combined it with your professional skill set to find your strengths and organise your work around them.

- Specified your worst-case scenarios and harnessed them to propel you in the opposite direction.

- Decided what your ideal lifestyle looks like today and

tomorrow and filtered your money out to take advantage
of both.

- Set up a Cash Hub, and redirected all your ongoing
  liabilities to a Fixed Cost Bucket.

- Sent yourself a specific amount to spend guilt free
  each week.

- Paying any debt down actively instead of simply accepting the minimum repayments.

Considering these steps are probably more in-depth than you
thought you were in for when you started reading, by this stage
you deserve a reward. If you have more direction in life and feel
less pressure to bring in cash each week after getting your financial house in order, this will buy you more time. Fewer distractions and less decision fatigue equal better results, which equals
more bargaining power at your job[48] or in your own business.

And to top it all off, having an amount put aside purely to ensure you have something to look forward to every twelve months
makes the Five Bucket system even more worthwhile.

---

48 / This bargaining power is what you use to get flexible working hours, a promotion,
a pay rise, a choice of which projects to work on, or to move departments within a company to something that fits your strengths better.

TAKE A HOLIDAY FROM YOUR MIND

In many ways, this entire book in centred on the concept of cognitive minimalism. The idea is that modern day life requires so much our mental capacity, finding a way to push back against the constant requirement of making decisions can benefit you in every area of your life. The less you have to think about where your life is going, and the less you have to think about your money day to day, the more you can free your mind to focus on other things.

One of the best ways to achieve that freedom is to take a break from your own minutia. Getting away from it all is without a doubt one of the best ways to clarify your feelings on every area of your life from the professional to the relational to the personal.

A famous maxim says travel is the only thing you can spend your money on that makes you richer. What I think this message is trying to say is that a change in perspective is vital for your mental growth.

People spend a lot of money to remove themselves from their regular environment. When you travel, you are essentially escaping the need to think about what typically fills your mind. The benefits have less to do with taking an awesome selfie in front of the Colosseum, and more to do with not having to worry about paperwork.

Taking time off mentally once a year to allow yourself the ability to examine the direction of your life will benefit you more than endless cocktails on a tropical beach – though I wouldn't discount those daiquiris entirely.

EMERGENCIES

Planning how you can use your Lifestyle Bucket is a lot of fun, but this account also doubles for unforeseeable events. Some choose to call it a 'Plan B'. So while this amount of money will enable you to have the time of your life ninety-nine times out of a hundred, it also has your back in case of an emergency.

On the slight chance that you need it, this money can be used in an instant to handle immediate problems. For example, insurance doesn't cover minor issues. If you can't work for a month due to sickness or accident and have to handle medical bills, having an amount sitting there ready to go can be extremely handy.

And without going too deep down this path, it's not getting hit by a bus that you should be looking out for. The majority of problems come from faults in your cell replication. In fact, only 3% of income protection payouts are due to accidents[49]. Even as a world-class bus dodger, there's a lot less you can do consciously on a genetic level.

So even assuming you're properly insured, having enough money to cover basic living costs in the event of an emergency is again giving you one less thing to think about. What you don't want is a situation where you need to sell down an investment to pay for an unforeseeable event.

---

[49] / https://www.bt.com.au/kpi/BT-Insurance-KPI-Customer-Case-Studies-claim-stats.pdf

LAST-MINUTE LIFE SAVER

The final unsung hero of the Lifestyle Bucket is the opportunity to use this money for anything. Let's say, for example, twelve months into a spending plan you change your mind, and instead of flying to Mexico, something else pops up that now has your attention.

Guess what? You have a lump sum of money to help you achieve it. I've learned to use travel as the motivator to grow this lump sum of cash, but the purpose of the money can – and often does – change.

I've had clients forgo flying to Berlin to purchase a Deus[50], chase a girl with an engagement ring instead of being chased by bulls in Spain, and purchase a property instead of backpacking through Asia.

Things change, opinions form with time, and priorities turn up. In other words, life happens. The beauty is creating room for options, whatever they may be. All that matters is that you are the one in the driver's seat.

And creating room for options is not about putting money aside for fixed costs. Fixed costs help you be comfortable on a daily basis, but serve no higher purpose. They're taken for granted. And it isn't about the money you spend each week. Spending money is for fun. Paying down debt gets you out of a bad place but doesn't move you forward, and wealth creation is about building an asset to replace your income when you can no longer work.

So give yourself room to move, room to get away from the daily grind. By directing a weekly amount to build up this account, you

50 / Just the greatest custom motorcycles in existence www.deuscustoms.com

put yourself in control of your money, not the other way around. At the very least, the ability to spend money however you like on an annual basis keeps you out of debt. Which we know by now, has many advantages.

The ultimate goal of this bucket strategy is to make your credit card obsolete. During the week you have your guilt-free spending money. And for those big annual expenses, whether they are well planned out or change last-minute, you now have your Lifestyle Bucket to take care of it.

REPROGRAMING BEHAVIOR

None of this is brain surgery, but there is some science behind it. What we are looking to achieve together is to change the relationship you have with your finance.

Currently, most people have an open relationship with their money – whether they realise it or not. They care for it; they want to keep it, but they don't really care who else has their hands on it.

If their fixed costs are high, and they don't have much control over their money, I like to point it out to them. Hence why I call it a reduction in salary. Once someone realises they are voluntarily opting in for a lower salary, the reality of fixing up their ongoing fixed costs becomes a higher priority.

Simply by repositioning the problem of fixed cost in a way that makes sense to my client, I take the emotion (and its ability to cloud judgement) out of the picture.

In the same way, this Lifestyle Bucket is simply a repositioning of the term 'short-term savings'. Remember, money is a highly emotional topic; in fact, it is one of the last taboo subjects in our culture. I have seen the results of repositioning money in people's mind, and it's amazing.

When we overwrite an existing thought with a new concept, our behaviour follows suit. It's not that simple though. The new concept has to be compelling if it is going to reshape our behaviour.

For example, 'short-term savings' is boring for two reasons. One, the term is not personalised. If I don't have a clear picture of how I will use the money, I won't see the consequence of dipping into it. The second reason is, who cares about savings? No one. The term is excruciatingly dull. I've worked with money long enough to tell you upfront, if you're using the term 'savings', please accept my apology in advance as I fall asleep.

Instead, use terms that connect the purpose with the action. Why are you filtering the money in the first place? Then ideally take it out of your hands. In the case of the Lifestyle Bucket, the best results have followed those who named the bucket after its exact purpose. People don't want savings; they want what they are saving for.

By using the Five Bucket Method, you can spend money now, spend it on something big every twelve months, and build long-term investments. All without the ongoing need to think about it multiple times a day.

Imagine being able to jump on a plane for a four-week vacation to New York. You board the plane having paid for it without a credit card, spending money each day however you like, guilt free, all the while your bills back home are being paid on time without you having to worry about it. Not only are you going to have a fantastic time, but it's also not going to cause any financial issues, and the benefit to your mind is going to be maximised.

On top of all this, as you'll see in the next chapter, your long-term assets will be building in favourable tax structures, allowing you the ability to live your ideal lifestyle in the future also.

The bucket system works so well because it takes you out of the centre of your financial life. With billions of dollars spent by the world's largest corporations on trying to figure out how to take up more of your time, outsourcing your financial life to automation is one of the best decisions you can make to be in control again.

Free up your mind, free up your attention, become more efficient, get better results, and utilise the bucket system in this book. If you can remove yourself from daily financial decisions, your success rate in every other area of your life will go up.

CHAPTER SUMMARY

....

Q *How this helps fund your ideal lifestyle?*

This step rewards you for all the hard work you have put in. If you have set time aside to consider what your ideal lifestyle looks like, then you have a responsibility to yourself to make it happen. By putting money aside for big annual expenses, you will be able to hit the items on your bucket list. It also doubles as an emergency fund in case you need a larger amount of money within a twenty-four hour period.

Q *How to make this easy?*

Name the bucket after the exact target you are aiming to achieve. Don't call it short-term savings or anything non-specific. If you have a plan to travel to Japan, call it 'Japan Bucket', if you plan on saving for a home call it 'Home Deposit'.

The power is in framing the plan and tracking your progress. The trickiest part of building this bucket is starting. Thankfully having an automated system transferring money in the background separates you from this hurdle.

The second hardest part is resisting the temptation to dip into it the moment it has any money in there. The most common phrases I hear are, 'I've never had that much in savings before in my whole life,' or, 'I need some of it for _____.' By connecting the name of the bucket with the desired outcome you are looking for, you are far less likely to touch it.

When you beat these two hurdles, something changes. I can't quite describe what it is. Calling it a 'change in habit' doesn't quite get there. It's a strange sense of protection that suddenly appears. As the amount grows in the background, you will start to realise what you have already achieved, and won't want to break the momentum. I've seen it a few times now. It's quite amazing to see someone go from never having any money in the bank to feeling proud of the amount that is there in the space of a couple of weeks – and doing whatever they can to defend it and build on it.

TEN

BUILDING YOUR FUTURE

THE INVESTMENT BUCKET

"WHEN I WAS YOUNG I THOUGHT
MONEY WAS THE MOST IMPORTANT THING IN LIFE;
NOW THAT I AM OLD, I KNOW IT IS."

- OSCAR WILDE

"THE BEST WAY TO PREDICT YOUR FUTURE
IS TO CREATE IT."

- ABRAHAM LINCOLN

uring the late 2000's in my days as a cage dwelling, button pushing, propeller-headed tax accountant, I would try to get some excitement in my life by day trading speculative stocks. And I did pretty well too.

I discovered early on a subset of equities traded on a daily basis called 'speculative shares' (*speccy* for short) which were earning zero income but were still traded like a game of cat and mouse. Thousands of dollars lined up on both sides of the buy and sell, waiting for someone to capitulate.

These equities would just sit there for months or years on end with nothing happening and then all of a sudden they would explode in value off the back of news stories that shined the light on a particular stock. And it didn't have to be the mainstream media; it could be a small post on a forum or research collated by a guy sitting in his basement sending his thoughts to his mailing list. As soon as these stocks piqued the interest of enough people, they would move. Often hundreds to thousands of percentage points in a mere matter of seconds.

This crazy world of violent fluctuations was where I figured out that someone like me, at the time without much capital backing, could make a lot of money if I played the game right.

So I began tracking a couple of tip sheets creating massive impacts to these speccy stocks. If you're unaware of what a tip sheet does, it works like this: you pay a stock tipping expert a couple of hundred dollars a year to receive their research. The crazy part was, it didn't matter if the research was legitimate or not. Any stock that got mentioned moved fast.

I signed up to a couple of these tip sheets, and my monthly stock tip would come in. From the moment that email was sent out by the author, it was a free-for-all to get in before the other subscribers and the momentum traders[51] jumped in. That meant I had a thirty-second window to get in before the stock blew up.

It was in this environment that I earned a thousand dollars in a day for the first time. And it was such a sweet win. After tracking a particular tip sheet for around six months, I realised this particular one turned up on the same day, at the same time every month. It was a pattern I hadn't noticed initially, but looking back through my old sheets I could see that it was unwaveringly consistent.

After realising I could predict this particular tip sheet down to the minute each month, I realised I could almost guarantee that I'd buy within the 30-second window. As such, this opportunity became the most important minute of my month, and like clockwork, it turned up as expected. I knew I was in early, so with every cent I had, I purchased the stock pick and started hitting the price refresh button with fervour as the price skyrocketed with all the other traders buying in after me.

With every press of the refresh button, the stock was up another 20%. It was crazy! After holding the stock for a total of around sixty seconds, I sold it again. And there, sitting in my account, was an additional $3,000 I didn't have only a minute prior.

I'd earned my monthly after tax salary at the time with one minute's work.

I thought I was the smartest person in the world. That night I

---

51 / Momentum traders have software that notice spikes in trading volume, and are designed to buy into these trades as early as possible to ride the wave up, and sell out in a short period of time to other traders looking to buy in also.

went out with my mates, paid for all the drinks, and figured I was only months away from spending the rest of my life as a full-time day trader.

The next month I had the same success and paid for some international travel. Things were going swimmingly! I was on the verge of quitting my job to pursue day trading full time. But as with the case of most things, easy come, easy go.

On the third month of my new trading system, I ramped up my leverage, my expectations for profit, and my adrenaline. Except, the tip sheet came in a half hour early and caught me off guard. Convinced at this stage that I was an infallible investing genius, I decided I could still make the system work. I didn't want to wait another month to get my next cash influx.

So like Pavlov's Dog, conditioned to salivate the moment the monthly stock tip dropped into my email, I starting hitting the same buttons to which I had grown accustomed. The problem was, I was late. I knew it, but I executed anyway. And I lost. Big. My previous two-month gains were gone.

The experience taught me investing is not speculating. There are always going to be ways to make money through investing, but the real money gets made through diligently putting aside an amount of money every week and investing in a high quality, value-driven, diversified portfolio.

THE PURPOSE OF YOUR INVESTING

The purpose of investments is to provide yourself with an income for when you no longer work. Its sole purpose is to fund your ideal lifestyle in the future.

This fact gets lost on most people. Most people think investing is to 'make more money', or to 'get rich'. But the truth is unless you have a lot of money upfront to invest, you're not going to make much from investments.

At least, that applies to the short term. Over the long term, it's a different story. In the long run, regular deposits put aside over decades, coupled with the power of compounding, – will give your investments the time and space to make you money.

But do you see the difference? One is short term, and one is long term. One perspective is 'to make more money', the other is that investments take decades to grow.

Because of this, before you start putting money aside, be very clear on the outcome you want. We will get to more on why this is important later, but the main point is to understand the only purpose of building a portfolio of investments is to provide yourself with an income when you no longer work.

Over a long enough period, we know investments go up, and dividends get paid, but there is next to no chance of timing the market to make sure you get it right in the short term. As such, you want to be thinking in terms of a long timeframe. If your timeline for investing is under five years, you're better off doing nothing and sitting in cash.

A lengthy timeline is a security measure. For example, if you were to pick the worst time in the last twenty years to invest

$100,000, say at the height of the market in October 2007, you were back ahead in 2013.[52]

Therefore building an investment portfolio requires two things, owning high-quality, diversified assets, and time. High-risk investments such as Angel investing and options trading take knowledge, skill, discipline and hard work. A regular investment portfolio doesn't. It needs diversification and time.

Now you have a better understanding of how to build a diversified portfolio, and what it's purpose is, I'm going to show you how easy it is to get distracted. These next few points show some common thinking patterns that get people into trouble.

EASY COME, EASY GO

The skill of holding on to money is learned, developed over time. And it's a valuable skill. Think about the countless people who have won the lottery over time, only to end up in situations worse than before they bought the ticket.

Instant wealth is typically very hard to keep. Because the acquisition was easy, the automatic internal theory is that it will be easy to replicate.

And herein lies the hidden benefit of building an investment portfolio over the course of a few decades. Long-term diligence also develops the additional required skill to hold on to that money for as long as possible.

---

52 / The Dow Jones was above it's pre-GFC 2007 height by 2013, and the Australian Accumulation index which includes reinvesting all dividends was higher than it's pre-GFC 2007 height by 2013 also.

Compare that to the concept of coming into a substantial amount of money in a short amount of time with little to no effort. Be that through inheritance or winning the lottery.

The statistics show, money provided to an individual with little to no regard to how it was made, often accompanies a poor respect for and a poor usage of the money. Indeed, almost half of all Lotto winners are broke within five years[53].

That is why actively putting an amount aside on a regular basis to the investment bucket is a lesson in not just building an investment portfolio, but vicariously learning the habit of holding on to it also.

In fact, inter-generational wealth is considered to have a high risk of failing due to this concept. While the first generation works extremely hard to provide a better life for their family and hands those values down to their children, it rarely makes it way to the third generation.

The second generation knows the sacrifice their parents made to create the wealth, and while not personally making the sacrifice, they have at least witnessed their parents' hard work and diligence. As a result, the second generation usually works hard to continue the success of their parents.

However, by the third generation, things become a little stranger. By this stage, the grandparents who created the money are the patriarchs and matriarchs of a family with a decent amount of money. Everyone owns their home, and they have money to spare.

This third generation has all of the benefit and none of the hard

---

53 / http://fortune.com/2016/01/15/powerball-lottery-winners/

work. Their parents weren't the ones to pull the family up from poverty, so there isn't the pressure to succeed that the second generation felt.

Ultimately, the third generation has a very sweet ride. They get all the benefits of wealth with none of the sacrifice. Is it any wonder then if they don't value their money in the same way as their parents and grandparents?

And that is the issue with having access to substantial amounts of money without the additional hurdle of having to respect it. This concept that money comes easy without responsibility is the exact reason money typically only survives inter-generationally for three generations.

It is why I believe in slowly filtering money aside to build a diversified portfolio, which in turn develops the character needed to hold on to money for the long term. Not only will it provide you with an income for your future when you no longer work, but it also gives birth to the self-discipline needed to ensure the longevity of the money in retirement.

KEEP MORE OF WHAT YOU WORKED FOR

The Investment Bucket represents your ideal lifestyle tomorrow. And while living your ideal lifestyle today is a major focus, ensuring that you live your ideal lifestyle in the future is the other half of the story.

As I've already written, the earlier you start, the easier it is to get ahead; but regardless of where you are on the accumulation journey, filtering out money to take care of your future is a massive part of living your ideal lifestyle.

Putting money aside each week is the one thing you can control to make sure you have an income in the future. While you can't control investment returns, you do have control over how much you put aside for your long-term plans.

And there are a couple of ways to do this. We will go into a few more specific strategies in Section III of this book, but at a high level you can build savings and investments in a horrible tax entity – your name – or you can grow the same assets in a far better tax environment. In other words: earning a greater return without taking on greater investment risk.

But before we get to any further information around tax structuring, let's have a look at where you can invest your money. We will dive into this a bit more in the following chapters, so let's examine the most common types of assets here first.

PROPERTY VS EQUITIES

First let's examine purchasing property, a very common investment in the western world. The 'bricks and mortar' argument has been around as long as I can remember.

Property as an investment has burrowed itself deep into the psyche of the western world – and for a good reason. Considering how emotional the topic of money is, owning property gives investors two appealing features not found with equities: transparency and control.

You can see property. You can touch it. You know who is renting the space; you know the management company that is looking after it for you. You know exactly how much is coming in from rent each month, and how much is going out in expenses.

As you have transparency over every piece of the puzzle, you also have the ability to change anything you don't like. The investor is in charge. This argument alone makes buying property a very appealing investment opportunity. The fact that rent consistently goes up over time along with the value of the building itself makes it a hugely popular investment.

Equities, on the other hand, offer far less transparency and control. Why? Unlike property, you no longer own and run the asset by yourself. Instead, you own a tiny fraction in a publically run company. As such, this degree of separation from the asset offers a far lower level of transparency and control.

These lower levels of transparency and control then directly convert into an aversion away from equities. Even though equities and property have essentially earned the same returns over the last thirty to forty years, many investors tend to favour one or the other.

Both investments provide growth. Both investments can be leveraged. Both investments provide income, and both present unique tax advantages54. As such, a healthy diversified portfolio should

---

54 / Property provides an excellent tax advantage called depreciation where you can claim the 'loss' of value to a building as it has aged as a tax deduction. This is only an accounting measure though. The value of the property would normally go up. Equities have an excellent tax advantage called 'franked dividends' where the company you own a share in first pays the tax on the income you receive, thereby reducing the amount of tax you have to pay on the income.

contain both, not just one or the other. This is to ensure your portfolio is stabilised during times of volatility in the respective asset classes.

CHAPTER SUMMARY

Q How this helps fund your ideal lifestyle?

The sole purpose of investments is to provide you with an income when you no longer work. While you can't control what returns you will receive, you can control how much you put aside to ensure you can live your ideal lifestyle in the future.

Q How to make this easy?

Start small, start early, and have the amounts put aside via automation so you don't have to make the decision to invest each week.

STE
PURO
CAPITA

EP 3
PHASE
ASSETS

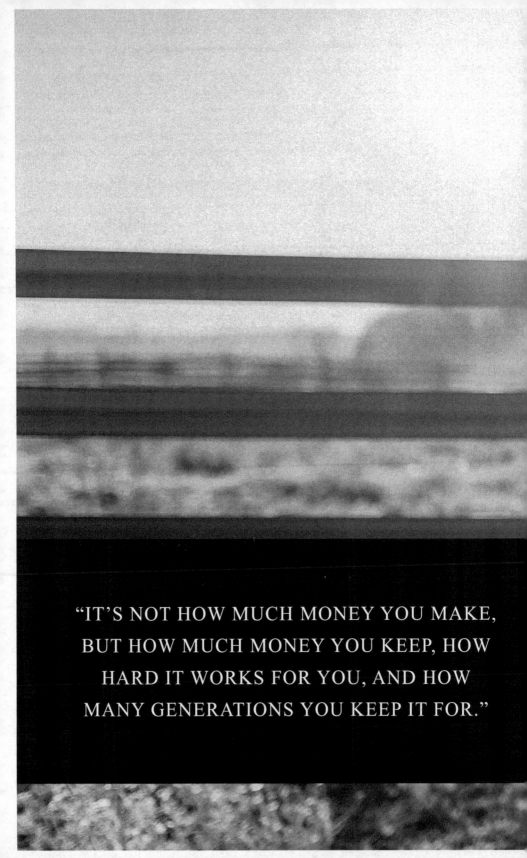

"IT'S NOT HOW MUCH MONEY YOU MAKE, BUT HOW MUCH MONEY YOU KEEP, HOW HARD IT WORKS FOR YOU, AND HOW MANY GENERATIONS YOU KEEP IT FOR."

- ROBERT KIYOSAKI

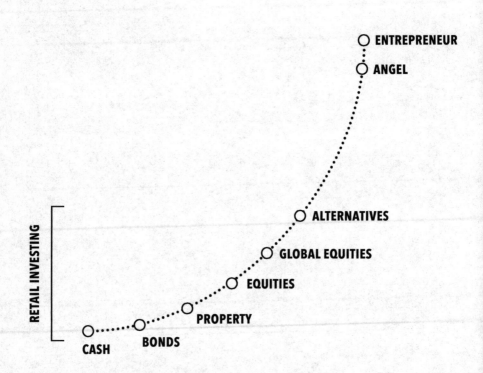

RETAIL INVESTING

CASH

BONDS

PROPERTY

EQUITIES

GLOBAL EQUITIES

ALTERNATIVES

ANGEL

ENTREPRENEUR

PURCHASING CAPITAL ASSETS

Purchasing capital assets is the third and final step in the three-step framework for a specific reason: the sole purpose of investing is to provide an income for your ideal lifestyle in the future when you no longer work. Assuming you still have a few years until that happens, you are better off getting the other two steps in place to ensure you have the longevity to create wealth.

This chapter covers how to build assets, but most importantly it focuses on the purpose of investing. Its fundamental principles being: don't lose money, don't get emotionally involved with your investing, and create an automated way to invest on an on-going basis without much input.

ELEVEN

FIRST RULE OF INVESTING

NEVER LOSE MONEY

"RULE NO.1: NEVER LOSE MONEY. RULE NO.2:
NEVER FORGET RULE NO.1."

- WARREN BUFFETT

"THERE SEEMS TO BE AN UNWRITTEN RULE ON WALL
STREET: IF YOU DON'T UNDERSTAND IT,
THEN PUT YOUR LIFE SAVINGS INTO IT."

- PETER LYNCH

f you rewind back to 2007 when I was just starting out in taxation, a woman in her late fifties came into my office to have her tax return completed.

She reluctantly took out her information, and with a scowl on her face told me to 'do what you can'. Me being both a little inexperienced and a little confused at her demeanour, took her paperwork and inputted her data into the program without any further small talk.

It turns out this woman was no longer working because she didn't need to. Looking over her paperwork, I realised she had inherited five properties twelve months prior with no mortgages attached. Her total income earned over the financial year was entirely from these properties she was now renting out to tenants.

The moment she came into this inheritance she decided to quit work altogether as her rental income was higher than her salary had ever been. Overnight she went from a struggling middle-aged woman to a successful investor.

After I had entered all income and deductions, we arrived at a tax payable of around $20,000. On my end, I thought it was pretty standard, considering whether you earn money through employment or investment income, there's always tax to pay.

She, however, did not see it this way. She thought the government was being unfair and was not very happy. I initially had some sympathy for her based on the fact she had not prepared to pay the tax, but then these words dropped out of her mouth: 'I wish I never owned these properties'.

My jaw hit the desk. This woman didn't care about the fact that she never had to work again because someone else set up a fantastic paying investment, all she cared about was the tax. At this moment I realised, just because someone owns investments, it does not mean they know what they're doing. It takes more than the ownership of assets to be a successful investor.

GYM MEMBERSHIPS DON'T MAKE YOU FIT

Have you known someone, or maybe you're guilty of this yourself, paying for a gym membership and never using it? I know I do. It's as though just owning a gym membership is enough to get results rather than putting in the hard work.

In the same way, holding investments doesn't automatically make you rich either. Whether you invest poorly or slack off on your fitness routine, you will experience the results reflective of the effort you put in.

For example, if you don't have a due diligence process and end up purchasing an investment that costs you money to hold on to, you're relying on hope to make money. You're a Hope Investor.

Hope investing has the unpredictable reputation of making some people a lot of money, and making others broke. As such I prefer the concept of owning an investment portfolio that pays an income instead.

Many a persuasive salesman has waded into the world of finance and investing with no intention of making you money. That's why it's important to have a due diligence process when buying assets, and the best due diligence you can have is to ensure the asset pays you from day one.

There is little point in starting to build an investment portfolio unless you have a plan. Don't be the kind of person who pays for a gym membership and hopes to get into shape. Don't be the type of investor who purchases an asset that does not earn an income, and relies on hope investing to make money.

RISKY BUSINESS

So what goes into a diversified portfolio? Well, that depends on how much risk you're comfortable with taking on. And that's why you need to know your Risk Profile[55].

Your Risk Profile dictates what percentage of your investment portfolio should be invested in Growth Assets, and what percentage should be invested in Conservative Assets[56].

There is no point having an aggressive portfolio if the ups and downs keep you up at night wanting to buy, sell, and change investment strategies because the news headline that morning screamed, 'Ten billion wiped off the markets'[57]. Long term in-

---

55 / Complete a free risk profile questionnaire here with Vanguard. The asset allocation recommendations are very simplified, however it is a good introduction. https://personal.vanguard.com/us/FundsInvQuestionnaire.

56 / Growth Assets are equities and property. Conservative Assets are cash and bonds. More in next chapter.

57 / Of course you're aware media companies share doomsday headlines to sell more product, but I'll make something very clear. Whenever you read this headline, remember the market silently earned that money in the past, it will again in the future. Don't stress. Chill.

vesting comes with ups and downs; the trick is to not care[58].

The more risk you are happy to take on as an investor, the more aggressive your Risk Profile will be, and the higher the percentage of Growth Assets should make up your investment portfolio. The less happy you are to take on risk as an investor, the more conservative your Risk Profile will be, and the higher the percentage of Conservative Assets should make up your investment portfolio.

In the end, you should have different asset allocations for different investment horizons. For example, if you are saving for a house deposit and plan on buying within five years, cash is a good option.

If you are building long-term wealth to replace your income when you no longer work in thirty years, a riskier asset allocation would be appropriate.

The idea is to know why you are putting money aside, and invest in the appropriate way. If you're buying a home, stay safe, and if you are building an investment portfolio, remember that it isn't so you can buy a new car in three years. It's so you can pay yourself an income when you no longer work.

So take your focus off investing. You shouldn't be distracting yourself or causing yourself decision fatigue. Don't try to time the market. Don't try to get fancy. You're either saving for a home in cash or building a long-term investment portfolio. It's not sexy, but then, it's not meant to be either.

---

58 / There is one caveat. If you have a high percentage of Growth Assets in your investment portfolio and you're within seven years of retiring — firstly — go get yourself a book more age-appropriate you geriatric (kidding :), and secondly it's worth taking some risk off the table. Seriously, if that's you, go check it out, it's called Sequencing Risk.

YOU'RE TOO EMOTIONALLY INVOLVED

There are investors, who despite having long-term investment plans, toss everything out the window as soon as there is a hiccup in the market because they're overly emotionally involved with their money.

Sure, it's one thing to be close to retirement and concerned about sequencing risk, but if you are young, and the market has a down-turn, why not copy the ultra-wealthy and use it as a buying oppor-tunity with the assets all being technically cheaper?

The last thing you want to do is chop and change investments on a regular basis. Why? Well, this should all be on automatic. What is the point in freeing you mind up by outsourcing and automating your cash flow, only to get bogged down with your investments?

And market timing is next to impossible. If you've seen the movie The Big Short, you know there are always going to be the lucky ones who get it right, but for the handful that do, there are thousands who get it wrong. Given a long enough time, any doomsday-er can be correct[59].

Just as you can't read the future, the majority of investors take the hit on the way down and sell out, and rarely buy back in on the rebound – the result being they end up losing more than if they had just stayed in the market[60].

If you have made the decision to invest for a certain time frame,

---

59 / Except for those cloistered cults who claim the return of Jesus/aliens/Elvis etc. They have an impressive unbroken 100% record of failure.

60 / Check out the research here http://www.schwab.com/public/schwab/nn/articles/ Does-Market-Timing-Work

and you have either done your due diligence or outsourced that due diligence to someone else[61], suck it up when there is a downturn, put your big boy/girl pants on and stay at the party. Once again, assuming you have quality investments, don't crystallise your losses – look to capitalise on a buyer's market.

THE NEXT BIG THING

One of the more humorous mistakes I see people make is this concept of the 'next big thing'. Many times, someone has walked into my office and let me know about an article they've read, a hot stock tip from a friend of a friend, or how a particular suburb is going to blow up in value soon. They're then shocked to learn that I'm not interested.

This concept of always chasing new and more exciting investment opportunities can be more fun than a diversified portfolio, but the goal of investing is not adventure; it's to build an asset base to fund your ideal lifestyle once you're no longer working.

Sure, some people have fun with investing, and if you're the type of personality who gets a thrill from trying to pick a winner, put a few dollars aside and do your best, but don't build an investment strategy around it. Your future self won't appreciate the cavalier investment strategy.

I've even had competitions in the past with clients to see who does

61 / A buyers agent can help find good properties, a stock broker or an online tip sheet can help with stock selection, an ETF can invest in market indices, and a financial adviser can help with managed funds.

better – me with my array of active and passive investments[62], or them with their speculative mining and pharmaceutical stocks.

I can't throw too much blame; I used to be the same way. I just have lived the exhausting experience of making and losing too much money this way. The updates flood in when things are going well, then they go quiet for a while again. Speculating can be fun, but it is not investing.

ASSET CLASS OBSESSION

One thing that makes me feel slightly uncomfortable is when someone has an intense obsession with a particular asset class and puts all their eggs in one basket.

The concept of building a property portfolio or an equities portfolio is faulty thinking. The Noble Prize winning investment theory called Modern Portfolio Theory[63] shows asset allocation brings in 90% of all returns.

This theory suggests 90% of the returns earned by an investment portfolio is made by simply being invested, rather than picking a winner like 'the right property' or 'the right equity'. As such, spending your time researching what to buy and sell is just another distraction causing you decision fatigue, and reducing your

62 / Active is when investment selection decisions are made by human investment managers. Passive is when those decisions are made by computer algorithms.

63 / Modern Portfolio Theory was created by American economist Harry Max Markowitz. He received the 1990 Nobel Memorial Prize in Economic Sciences for his research promoting asset allocation rather than specific asset picking as the main driver of growth. There exists arguments for and against this theory. My opinion rests with the greatest investor of all time – Warren Buffet. He's a big fan.

performance in all other areas of your life.

If you are invested in property, and the market goes up, you're going to make money regardless of how much research went into your property. If you're in equities, and the whole market drops, you're going to lose money regardless of how much research went into your stock selection.

That is why it's dangerous to have an obsession with a particular asset class. Especially if you are leveraged. If your asset class of choice goes through a tough time, you may be forced to sell at the worst time possible.

It should never be only property or equity investing. It should be both. Because, as the first rule of investing is not to lose money, an investor needs to focus on owning a diversified portfolio and avoid being over-exposed to the risk of having all their eggs in one basket.

Having favourites with something reasonable like sports teams is understandable, but having favourite asset classes in invest-ing will just get you into trouble. If you have all your assets in one asset class, when the inevitable downturn happens you may struggle to remain liquid and then be forced to sell at the worst time possible.

TO OUTSOURCE OR NOT TO OUTSOURCE

Reading over those common mistakes will evoke one of two emotions. Either a) you're well versed in investments and feel comfortable enough to make your investment purchases or b) you've read the above mistakes and now want nothing to do with your asset purchasing decisions.

Thankfully, there are people and products available to help make investment decisions easy. So here we decide if you should manage your investments by yourself or not. Needless to say, if you're confident you have a due diligence process to ensure that you purchase high-quality investments, go for it. If you're not sure, you should look to outsource.

If you want help with purchasing a property, a Buyers Agent can help. Generally, Buyers Agents have worked as Real Estate agents in the past and now use their skills to find and buy property for investors. If you want help with equities, you have the option to pay for investment selection advice from a Stock Broker, an online tip sheet or a Financial Adviser. Alternatively, you can use a financial product.

Financial products purchase investments for an ongoing percentage cost of 0.05% all the way up to 5% of your invested amount. Obviously, the higher the fee, the greater effect it will have on your wealth creating ability, so looking for cost effectiveness is important, however like most things cheaper is not always better. Let's see what causes these higher and lower ongoing costs.

1   *Active management (higher cost) versus Passive management (lower cost).* The cost differences match the investment philosophy differences. Active management employs teams of financial analysts to pour through annual reports, meet with CEO's, perform due diligence and create investment recommendations for senior partners to decide whether they will purchase a particular investment. Active management is labour intensive and comes with a corre-

sponding cost. Passive investments, on the other hand, are completed by algorithms. No need for humans to do the research, because computers do all the work – which is reflected in the lower cost. The investment strategies are generally far simpler, but again according to Modern Portfolio Theory, this won't have much an effect on the performance outcome.

2   *The complexity of the investments.* Some investments are very easy to access, for example depositing money into a bank. Some investments are very complex such as purchasing options to hedge against an existing portfolio of international bonds. The more complexity involved, and time needed to complete these transactions, the higher the ongoing cost.

3   *Whether commissions are paid to a third party.* Some investments have an ongoing fee paid to the third party who sold the financial product in the first place. It is this point in particular that has many people uninterested in financial products. However, there are a couple of things to note. A law was recently introduced in Australia making it illegal to pay commissions on all new financial product investments. This is important to know, as any new financial product investments you purchase won't have commissions attached, and you can ask the product provider to remove commissions on any existing financial product investments.

Active management was once the golden child of diversified portfolios, but after the Global Financial Crisis (GFC) people began asking what they were paying for. From 2008 onwards, the overwhelming amount of new financial product investments has been ETF (exchange-traded fund) passive investments.

There is some solid research done by Vanguard who put forward a good argument[64] as to why Passive management outperforms the majority of active management, and new phone apps such as Acorns allow you to build a diversified portfolio without having to think about it, all from your smartphone.

In summary, if you're confident enough to purchase your property and equities go ahead. If you want a bit of help, you can hire a Buyers Agent for property, a Stock Broker for equities, or purchase financial products to access a diversified equities portfolio. If you want help with Risk Profile, asset allocation, Active and Passive financial product recommendations, and how it all works together to fund your ideal lifestyle in the future, then a Financial Adviser is the high touch investment solution.

---

64 / Vanguard, *'The case for index-fund investing'*, March 2015

CHAPTER SUMMARY

....

Q *How this helps fund your ideal lifestyle?*

Building a portfolio of assets to fund your ideal lifestyle in the future requires you to make sound investment decisions. To that end, building wealth takes a lot more than just buying a random asset and hoping it will go up in value. The first rule of investing is: never lose money.

Q *How to make this easy?*

Don't get distracted by the next big thing or a particular asset class because you have an emotional attachment to it. What you are after is a diversified portfolio of different asset classes that is easy to monitor and maintain, that isn't too expensive and doesn't need a lot of your attention.

Buyers Agents are great for finding the right property; Stock Brokers can help buy direct equities – but as I've said, according to Modern Portfolio Theory there isn't much value in trying to chase a 'winner.' Active and Passive financial products can allow you to purchase a diversified portfolio easily, and a Financial Adviser can put all the pieces of the puzzle together to ensure you have the best outcome.

If you decide you need help, the hardest part here is how to find good help. How do you know you have a good Buyers Agent or Financial Adviser? This question is unfortunately still very hard to answer for someone with a limited network in the finance industry. Experience is rarely a good indication of success, nor is the size of the fee you pay. 'Independence' is nothing more than a marketing spiel, and industry awards rarely reflect best client outcomes.

As such, www.adviserratings.com.au is a good place to start. From here you can meet with a handful of professionals and go with your gut feeling. What is right for you isn't going to be right for someone else, so it's hard for me to give blanket suggestions.

If you're stretching for any suggestions, then the only question I would want to see answered is: 'What are the inherent conflicts in your business model?' How honest that answer is could give you all the answers you need.

TWELVE

INVESTMENT GURUS STILL HAVE JOBS

WHY DIVERSIFICATION WORKS

"AN INVESTMENT IN KNOWLEDGE
PAYS THE BEST INTEREST."

- BENJAMIN FRANKLIN

✈

"A RISING TIDE LIFTS ALL BOATS."

- JOHN F. KENNEDY

ike most parents, mine did not enjoy the fact that, at seventeen, I was old enough to drive. In fact, my mother refused to teach me anything about driving. Her assumption was that, by limiting my experience, I would have no chance of passing the driving exam.

What she did not account for was my determination. Nothing was going to stand between me and that driver's license. And when I blitzed the test on the first attempt, she was left to ponder her strategy as her inexperienced son jumped behind the wheel of a car.

That small and liberating plastic card was my ticket to freedom. And no newly minted driving enthusiast is fully baptised into the ways of the motorist without the well-worn tradition of a road trip. So, on the very first weekend since earning my license, myself and a handful of mates headed to Byron Bay for the weekend.

I was old enough to drive, but I was still another eleven months and three weeks away from being able to buy alcohol. But how could our underage road trip be complete without underage drinking? Thankfully we had had a Sepo[65] mate who had a unique way of scoring us beer for the weekend.

In Australia, we write our dates in a very logical progression: Day/Month/Year. It makes sense as it's an ascending time interval similar to seconds: minutes: hours. Simple. Americans, on the other hand, choose to write their dates in the peculiar manner of Month/Day/Year.

---

65 / Sepo – A thoroughly Australian nickname for someone from the United States. The evolution being: Yankee/Yank/Septic Tank/Sepo. A term of endearment rather than menace.

This discrepancy worked in our favour. Our Sepo mate was born a year before us, but so late in the year as to warrant being in our grade at school. His birthdate on an Australian license would have looked something like 01/12/1982. However, it was written on his US license as 12/01/1982, making him appear to be almost a full year older. It was perfect.

This subtle yet significant difference in the dating methods cleared our final hurdle to freedom as minimum wage bottle shop employees aren't trained in the finer points of trans-pacific date displays. We filled the boot to the brim with enough bottles to impress Keith Richards[66] and left for Byron Bay.

Four young guys heading to Byron Bay on their first road trip calls for one thing: road beers. And with only a couple of hours into our trip, the inevitable happened: 'Clayton, pull over. We need to use the bathroom'.[67]

I pull over to the side of the highway where they had less privacy than the Shibuya intersection[68], and everyone proceeded to empty their bladders. Mission accomplished, they jumped back into the car, only to find out that my engine wouldn't start.

Now, these days there are virtual roadside assistants connected to in-car wifi and all other kinds of luxuries. A 1979 Toyota Corona, on the other hand, needs more of an elbow-grease kind of assistance.

---

66 / Clearly not accurate, but enough to get four teenage boys drunk for a weekend. By that I mean we had a six-pack.

67 / My rose tinted glasses have made this drunk sixteen year old sound far more polite than he actually was.

68 / Busiest pedestrian intersection in the world located in the Tokyo suburb of Shibuya.

So there we were, broken down on the side of the road with the combined mechanical skills of a six-year-old with his first Tonka Truck[69], when a guy in a white Kombi van pulled over to see what's up.

Now this guy had an awesome vehicle (tick one for mechanic skills). He had that casual throw-about nature which only comes with working blue collar jobs for a while (tick two for mechanic skills), and he also had the kind of hands that could strangle a bear (tick three, we have ourselves a saviour).

We popped the bonnet, and I jumped in the car to turn it over. He took a quick look, and casually asked, 'Do you have a metal file in the boot?' Ridiculously, I did. I handed it to him, and he asked me to try the ignition again.

This time, he jammed the file into the starter engine and off she roared. Solved. Like a boss. He smiled, handed me the file, and jumped back into his car, leaving us all with a new man-crush, a resolution to learn a bit more about cars, and a start-up engine similar to those crank up T-Model Ford's.

Cars, in general, are embarrassingly completely out of my zone of expertise. Luckily for us, the legendary Kombi Man was there to help us out. And even though he saved our inaugural road trip, there were a few ways we could have restarted the car and got ourselves back on the road.

His method was one in the sea of car fixing strategies. It worked, but many could have. He served a very specific purpose at a very

---

69 / I'm going to assume here for a second you are aware of how unbelievably amazing Tonka Trucks are to a six year old. In saying that, apparently it does absolutely nothing to help improve real world mechanic skills.

specific time, but jamming a metal file into a starting engine is not the answer to every mechanical problem. Nor would it have been my first choice.

In the same way, until such time you feel comfortable investing on your own, you're going to need help from investment 'Kombi Man's' along the way.

Even still, these experts are going to have their own biases and slants, so ultimately it is up to you to ensure you are getting the best outcome. And the easiest, simplest, most researched and empirically proven way to do this is by having a diversified portfolio.

CAT AND DOG PEOPLE

Diversification is the strategy of investing in many different asset classes[70] to minimise volatility. The idea is by avoiding an 'all eggs in one basket' approach, when things do suddenly go wrong as they have in the past and they will again in the future, you won't be caught in a situation that forces you to sell down at a bad time.

Volatility can come from some unexpected places. Did you know that Americans not paying their mortgages en masse can affect you? Or why it should be your concern that the retirement age and benefits in Greece are overly generous? Well, those two factors caused such widespread issues the global economy is still struggling to get back to where it was a decade ago.

---

70 / Asset classes are groups of investments. For example 'equities', 'property', 'bonds', 'commodities' etc.

And the list of macro-economic events that can affect an investment portfolio is endless. It's impossible to fully understand every possible investment cause and effect going on around the whole world, and as such, the safest bet is to diversify the risk.

But people are people, and they get swayed by their emotions. They generally have an affinity for a particular type of asset class, and their reasoning for it can be anything. Maybe their parents preferred property, or they went to a seminar and learned about options trading.

These preferences give rise to 'property investors' or 'options traders'. These terms remind me of 'dog people' and 'cat people'. Neither is better than the other, but some people simply have an affinity for a particular choice.

The difference is, however, the cat/dog conundrum is polite dinner conversation and has no far-reaching consequences. Not diversifying your risk, on the other hand, can have catastrophic effects on your ability to live your ideal lifestyle in the future.

Let me explain the faulty thinking that goes into believing any particular asset class is superior. It comes down to the fact that all gurus, regardless whether they are a property Buyers Agent, a Stock Broker, a Financial Adviser, or a Commodities Trader, earn more money from their employment than they do from their investments.

Let that sink in for a second. The simple fact is if picking 'the right equity' was a consistent way to make money, stockbrokers would only trade for themselves full time. They would do it from their hotel room in New York or Barcelona, and earn more money from their ability to trade the market than they would from employment.

In the same way, if property were the best investment, property Buyers Agents would just search and buy new houses from the internet while at home on their private beach, and live off the income.

The obvious indicator that no asset class is foolproof is the fact that the professionals paid to help select these investments still have jobs. Yet every month I meet someone who tells me they love a particular asset class.

Diversifying your asset classes is the best way to invest so you don't go under when your asset class of choice takes a dive. No asset classes are immune to ebbs and flows. If a rising tide lifts all boats, a falling tide brings them all back down again.

There will be times in your investment career where your favourite asset class will be the shining star and other times when it will tank, and then the others will prop you up. Investing isn't about being a dog person or a cat person; it's about building an asset base over an extended period to pay yourself an income for when you no longer work.

MODERN PORTFOLIO THEORY

So if the concept of building an 'all eggs in one basket' approach to asset building is faulty thinking, let's take a closer look at the Nobel Prize winning investment theory Modern Portfolio Theory[71].

Like all theories, it has its fair share of detractors who point out

71 / Modern Portfolio Theory is credited to the American economist Harry Max Markowitz. He received the 1990 Nobel Memorial Prize in Economic Sciences for his work which promotes asset allocation rather than specific asset picking as the main driver of growth.

that, despite best efforts, it is a fallacy to call markets rational, efficient or fair, which Modern Portfolio Theory requires in order to operate. These criticisms while being theoretically correct, are countered with studies showing asset allocation is responsible for around 90% of all investment returns[72].

While I'm sure to have been drunk enough at some stage to claim I was a Nobel Laureate, unfortunately, facts don't hold up that claim. As such, all I can do is assume this theory, as supported by additional research is correct. And if earning 90% of returns are earned by exposure to asset classes, the old maxim of 'time in the market rather than timing the market' is empirically true.

Put simply, by holding all the different asset classes you will make money when things go up, lose money when things go south, and be better for it over the long run.

I understand if all this sounds counterintuitive. Assets should be judged individually on their own merits. Apple, for example, should rise and fall on the amount iPhones they sell, not on whether the asset class called 'equities' is performing well.

And if you purchase the worst property on the best street, close to amenities and public transport, schools and shopping centres, all these factors should count towards the success of the investment. Not whether the property market is cooling down or taking off.

But the research does not support this. The research says to be in the right place at the right time with exposure to a particular asset class, and you will see the 90% of the gains. As such, don't focus your time on the last 10% by trying to 'pick a winner'.

72 / Again, Vanguard with their research to the rescue. https://personal.vanguard.com/pdf/s324.pdf

Instead, use your time to make sure you have exposure to every asset class.

HAVE A FINGER IN EVERY PIE

Now let's cover what types of asset classes are available to investors on the market today, and how to go about owning them. We will start with the most conservative and work our way up the risk-to-return spectrum.

CASH

The first asset class is the simplest of all of them: cash in the bank. The only option here is whether you hold your money in an 'at call' account, meaning it's available to you anytime, or whether it's held in a 'term deposit' and locked up for a set amount of time. Typically the term deposit gives you a minor additional increase in the interest rate.

ADVANTAGES:
- 'At call' money is easily accessible
- Easy to understand investment
- Safe investment

DISADVANTAGES:
- 'Term deposits' can lock your money up
- Small earning potential

ACCESS:
- I'm going to assume you know how to deposit money into a bank.

BONDS

The second asset class is less commonly known. It's called a Bond[73]. A Bond is a promise from a large institution such as a government or publically listed company to pay back money lent to them. You also receive income during the term they hold your money called a coupon.[74]

Of course, there's always the chance you won't ever see the money again. Just ask an Argentinian bondholder from 2001[75]. But generally, the risk of non-payment is low. The higher the perceived risk of not getting your money back, the higher the coupon you receive for taking on the risk.

ADVANTAGES:
- Typically a safe investment
- Earnings are a little above cash at bank
- Allows diversification with conservative assets

DISADVANTAGES:
- Have been hard to access in the past
- Typically have small earning potential
- Generally less understood
- Can still lose money despite perceived safety

---

73 / There are variations of Bonds called Credit and Fixed Interest (horrible names. I know), but they are all attempting to achieve the same thing. Provide income a little above the returns on cash for only a little more risk.

74 / 'Wait' I hear you say. 'Isn't a coupon used by fast food joints to attract broke uni students on a Tuesday night?' Why yes they are! But you know, on account of everything else being confusing in finance, why not give it a horrible name? Soon we plan on renaming 'money' to 'Little Green Men', and 'banks' will be known as 'Potatoes'.

75 / Argentina ran out of money to pay back the loans it took back in 2001. As at time of writing, those owed the money are still looking to get paid and the debt has not been resolved.

ACCESS:
- To access Bonds directly will cost you at least $50,000 and a good amount of investment sophistication to buy.
- The easiest and most diversified way is through a financial product such as a bond fund or ETF.

PROPERTY

The third asset class is property, a common investment that earns money for the investor in capital growth and rental income. Property is unique on this list of investments as you can personally improve the quality of the asset by repainting or installing a new letterbox to help raise rental income almost immediately.

ADVANTAGES:
- Very easy to understand asset class
- Can personally improve the value and income
- The investor has clarity over each moving part
- Typically been a good earning investment

DISADVANTAGES:
- Deposits require a large sum to get started
- Bad tenants can cost time and money
- Difficult to access money if you need it
- The large capital value makes it hard to own while maintaining a diversified portfolio

ACCESS:
- Directly through a real estate agent, or if you want advice, with the help of a Buyers Agent.

EQUITIES

The fourth asset class is Equities. Commonly known as Shares or Stocks, this asset class is traded on the securities exchange market. Each unit owned represents ownership of a tiny piece of the public company.

The quality of the equity can range from a massive multinational company earning billions of dollars per year (typically known as 'blue chips'), all the way down to a speculative mining stock where the total assets are a business name and a permit to fly over a patch of land to search for resources in the ground.

Equities pay an income to the investor every year from the company's profit called a dividend. The taxation on this type of income can be very attractive with Franking[76].

ADVANTAGES:
- Easy to purchase through broker
- No ongoing personal involvement required
- Typically been a good earning investment
- Can sell easily to access funds

---

[76] / Again, horrible name. No, a guy called Frank is not paying the tax for you. Company tax in Australia is around 30%. Because the government has said it doesn't want the investor to pay tax twice, fully franked dividends come with the 30% tax already applied. What this means is investors on the highest marginal tax rate will only pay around 15% on fully franked dividend income, and investors who receive the income in a 0% tax entity will actually receive the 30% tax paid as an additional income. More on 0% entities in the next chapter.

DISADVANTAGES:
- Some financial understanding required
- Typically more volatile than other investments

ACCESS:
- Through a low-cost online broker if you know what you want to buy.
- If you would like research and recommendations, use a full-service broker.
- ETF's can give access to an entire market easily

GLOBAL EQUITIES

This brings me to the fifth asset class of Global Equities. Some of the more obscure markets such as Bulgarian shares are hard to acquire77, but the major global equity markets are getting easier to access all the time.

ADVANTAGES:
- Access profitable companies in other countries
- Increase diversification with Growth Assets

DISADVANTAGES:
- Higher levels of financial understanding required
- Typically been hard to access in the past
- Can be highly volatile in emerging markets

77 / Because the demand for these obscure markets is not high enough, the technology to connect to these markets aren't developed yet.

ACCESS:

- You may need an international online broker if you want to purchase directly.
- A broker with access to Global Equities will need some research to find.
- Otherwise, a financial product such as a managed fund or ETF can make things easy.

ALTERNATIVES

Finally arriving at sixth is Alternative Assets. This group of lesser-known investments rise and fall independently from the more common investments above. Alternatives come in handy since, as we saw through the GFC when all the above asset classes took a hit.

To stimulate the economy[78], the government reduced interest rates creating less return for cash investors. Usually, this would increase the value of Bonds with investors pulling their money from the bank to purchase Bonds in search of better returns. However, many large companies struggled during the GFC, and their Bonds plummeted.

Equities, both in Australia and internationally, were hit hard, as were many pockets of real estate. However, due to government stimulation, and a lot of money coming from China by way of

---

78 / In times of financial crisis, the government has two levers it can pull to stimulate the economy. Stimulating the economy basically means ensuring the population continues to spend money and invest as our entire economy depends on it. The government can either reduce interest rates which in turn annoys cash investors enough to move their money from bank savings accounts into other investments such as equities, and they can give money to their citizens. During the GFC the Australian government did both.

mining on an institutional level, and property purchases on a personal investment level, the real estate market in Australia managed to hold up.

But what does this mean for the average investor? If everything goes down at the same time, how do you diversify out of that risk? This is where alternative assets play an important part of a diversified portfolio.

Gold, for example, is often laughed about as an investment as it's a dirty, bumpy piece of metal, dug up from the ground, cleaned, and melted into small pieces of metal, only to be buried in the ground again.

However, it's enjoyed such a close relationship to wealth over thousands of years, that purely through the passage of time, we simply accept it to be a store of wealth. Historically, as risk and volatility go up, gold has often surged in value, saving many diversified portfolios from disaster.

Other Alternative Assets are Hedge Funds. Hedge Funds were typically only for the rich and famous, but these days they can be purchased via financial products. The big advantage is they can trade options and still make money in a downturn.

ADVANTAGES:
- Investments can still go up in falling markets
- Provides even greater diversification

DISADVANTAGES:
- Higher levels of financial understanding required

- Typically been hard to access in the past
- Can compound losses if done incorrectly

ACCESS:

- Commodities such as oil, gold and agriculture are accessed via ETFs these days.
- Hedge funds are accessed directly or through financial products such as Managed Fund.

CHAPTER SUMMARY

....

Q *How this helps fund your ideal lifestyle?*

Having a diversified portfolio built steadily over many years will create the largest possible amount of money to provide you with an income when you no longer work to fund your ideal lifestyle in the future.

Avoiding the 'all your eggs in one basket' approach will ensure you are not overly exposed to any particular asset class during the inevitable downturns. The worst-case scenarios I have seen in my career are older investors who leveraged into non-diversified portfolios and lost everything during downturns.

Q *How to make this easy?*

Building a portfolio as profitable and as stable as possible involves diversification. It's not about finding the 'right property' or 'right equity', Nobel Prize winning research tells us simply being in the market across enough asset classes for a long enough time will have the best result.

As such, the easiest way to own a diversified portfolio is through financial products such as managed funds and ETFs. The only decision you have to make here is whether you want to pay for active management or pay less for passive management.

If you are convinced of the passive management theory, then

ETFs are purchased directly through a broker, either low cost online or full service. There are quite a lot to choose from these days. See http://www.asx.com.au/products/etf/managed-funds-etp-product-list.htm for a list.

Buying property can be a confusing and complicated affair. Often involving ridiculous amounts of paperwork, solicitors and accountants meetings and of course time. As such, a Buyers Agent can help with the initial purchase, and a good property manager can look after the property for you.

If you want someone to recommend a diversified portfolio, a Financial Adviser is your best bet. Remember, no new recommendations can have commissions attached. Every Financial Adviser has their investment philosophy, so it's impossible for me to comment on the possible outcomes, however, if they have a rigorous investment selection process that is a good start. You could always contact an adviser and ask for their investment philosophy and investment selection criteria before anything else.

Some advisers believe the passive argument entirely and will invest you solely in this. Others believe in the active management, not because of commissions but because of results. My philosophy is a 50/50 split between active and passive.

THIRTEEN

DON'T PUT YOUR HIP OUT

A LETTER TO YOUR FUTURE SELF

"INVESTING SHOULD BE MORE LIKE WATCHING
PAINT DRY OR WATCHING GRASS GROW.
IF YOU WANT EXCITEMENT, GO TO LAS VEGAS."

- PAUL SAMUELSON

················ ✈ ················

"THE QUESTION ISN'T AT WHAT AGE I WANT TO RETIRE,
IT'S AT WHAT INCOME."

- GEORGE FOREMAN

When I was learning about money for the first time in my early twenties, I concluded from the books I was reading that wealth gets created through investing. That all it would take to make millions of dollars was an excellent due diligence process. From there, I could pick the right investments and watch the money roll in.

Along with a whole bunch of other assumptions that dissipated the longer I worked with money, the realisation that no one made life changing money from investing was possibly the biggest shock of all.

The reason being investing is risky, and generally not all that profitable. Investing is great once you have money, but it's near on impossible to trade your way up from nothing to millions of dollars.

And this is why I make a point to teach that investing is not about making money, but rather a long-term project in diligence. Money consistently put aside to purchase diversified investments for the sole purpose of paying you an income when you no longer work is the only reason to invest.

And since the process of building wealth is as important as the quality of the investments you own, I make sure purchasing capital assets is the third and final step in the framework.

The first step is to clarify your ideal lifestyle. There is no point of working towards anything until you know what you're aiming for. The second step is to organise your cash flow to fund your plans today. Lastly is to put aside money to ensure you live your ideal lifestyle in the future also.

However in my experience as a financial adviser, I mostly meet people randomly invested in assets such as property and shares in some misdirected attempt to achieve the ethereal goal of 'being rich'. They have no real idea of what they are trying to achieve.

So I see countless advertisements on how to 'get rich' through day trading on social media, or complex investment strategies advertised on bus shelters. The unflattering thing about investing however, is it should be one of the most boring aspects of your life.

But boring doesn't sell, does it? Sexy sells. Getting rich sells. So people rush to purchase foreclosed homes in New Jersey, or a speculative pharmaceutical company with new 'life-changing technology'.

And it's not to say all of these investments are horrible, but a good investment doesn't need to be advertised with some hook to attract money. Good investments are sniffed out pretty quickly, and capacity quietly filled. If an investment is being advertised, it means smart money doesn't want it. That should ring an alarm bell.

So the purpose of investing is not about picking winners, or haphazardly heading out to the market and randomly buying assets. It's setting up a simple long-term plan, achieved via a regular automatic deposit into a diversified portfolio.

Now we can get to the most unsexy-sexy part of investing. If building wealth is only for later in life and needs diversification, how do you invest for better gains without taking on extra investment risk? The answer: by using an efficient tax entity to build your investment portfolio.

THE AUSTRALIAN OFFSHORE
BANK ACCOUNT

Creating wealth is a long-term process, and in the same way that being a small degree off-course can have a huge impact while navigating a long journey, small effects add up to big outcomes over long-term investing.

As such, tax efficient investing creates better returns for no extra risk. If you build the exact same assets in two separate entities, with the only difference being the tax rate applied to the earnings, the result will be better returns for the entity with the lower tax environment.

With that in mind there is a tax structure in Australia you can build assets in, so tax efficient it makes seeking a tax dodging strategy like an offshore bank account in the Isle of Man redundant.

Why risk either being ripped off or going to jail by syphoning your money offshore to avoid tax, when there is a perfectly legal way to do so right now?

Very few people understand how attractive this investment vehicle is, as it has a very boring and bureaucratic name. Considering the advantages of ending up with more money in your pocket over the long term, it's strange you never see this tax structure up in lights.

However, for those in the know, it has such unbelievable advantages that the government built restrictions on how much you can put in. They did so to stop those who bother to wade through the technical data from pouring as much money in as possible.

Lucky for you, I'm going to save you the hassle of peeling through hundreds of pages of dry government fact sheets, and instead put all the tax benefits here for you in plain English.

The crazy thing is, you would already have heard of this tax structure before, probably even own one, but found it to be as stimulating as a Top 40 dance track from the 1990's[79]. It's called Superannuation.

The misconception about Superannuation is that it's an investment. It isn't. It's a tax structure. Think of it as a car. Just as you can put any person in a car, you can build any kind[80] of investment portfolio inside of Superannuation.

It will save you money right now today, save money every year, and save money in retirement. Put simply, with the choice to build an investment portfolio in your own name, compared to building an identical portfolio in Superannuation, you can ensure a far better result by using a tax-efficient entity while not taking on additional investment risk[81].

---

79 / Except The Prodigy, they were awesome, and I won't hear another word about it.

80 / Allowed by the Superannuation Industry Supervision (SIS) Act. Basically most assets, except those you gain pleasure from ie. an old car or painting, or businesses you or your family own. This is a very short summary. Everything in more detail at https://www.legislation.gov.au/Details/C2016C00236, or talk to a Financial Adviser.

81 / While investment risk stays the same, legislative risk increases. Some people are concerned the government will one day commandeer all money inside of Superannuation. In my opinion, I don't see a free market society doing that.

1   SAVE MONEY TODAY

As an ex-tax accountant, I can't tell you how many people
ask this question around tax time: 'What can I do to reduce
my tax?' Most people hate paying more tax than they have
to, and will do anything to reduce it. Think Negative Gearing,
the purposeful loss in income to pay less tax.

What if there was a way to reduce your income, but rather
than losing your money through Negative Gearing, you kept
the money instead. Pay less tax, but keep the money instead
of losing it.

This strategy is called salary sacrifice. It is redirecting a portion of your salary to Superannuation and is taxed at 15%[82].
For example, if your salary is $200,000, you pay close to half
your income in taxes and levies[83]. By redirecting a portion of
your salary to long-term investments, you immediately save
34%[84] tax. Show me where else you can find a risk-free[85]
34% return.

2   SAVE MONEY EVERY YEAR

Investments should earn the investor income every year. If
you hold investments in your own name, this income goes on

82 / For those whose income is under $300,000 per year.

83 / Tax rate over $180,000 2015/2016 = 45% + 2% Medicare levy + 2% temporary
budget repair levy = 49%.

84 / To achieve a tax saving of 34% the calculation is 49% - 15% (superannuation
tax) = 34%

85 / Risk free as you don't have to invest this money to receive this benefit. You could
be 100% in cash inside of super and still get these tax benefits. All investments have
risk, but this strategy is a tax strategy, not an investment.

top of your salary. For example, if you earn $80,000 per year from employment, and a further $20,000 per year in investment income, the investment income is taxed at 39%[86].

If instead, you earned the $20,000 investment income inside of a Superannuation tax structure, you would have only paid 15% tax. Saving 24% tax on your investment returns every year of your wealth creation is going to have a substantial positive effect on your long-term results. Also, as franked dividends are taxed at 30%, and the tax environment for Superannuation is only 15%, you're able to claw back the other 15% tax from the government. Imagine that! The government paying you tax instead of the other way around!

3   SAVE MONEY IN THE FUTURE

The benefits of the Superannuation tax structure are impossible to beat once you hit the age you are finally going to start using your asset base for the purpose it was designed for: to pay you an income when you no longer work. It is impossible to beat because these three points have a tax rate of 0%. And you can't beat 0% tax. It's truly an offshore bank account within our own borders.

3A. SELL ASSETS FOR 0% CAPITAL GAINS TAX (CGT)

When a couple in their sixties is sitting in front of me and about to declare retirement, they often tell me with pride the size of the investment portfolio they have built up over the last forty years in their own names. Properties, shares, managed funds etc.

---

86 / Income between $80,000 - $180,000 is taxed at 2015/16 rates of 37% + 2% Medicare levy = 39%

The pain in their eyes when I tell them the size of their tax bill because of their success has stayed with me. It's not fun learning you have to pay the government hundreds of thousands of dollars just as you're about to start surviving on the spoils.

If they had only known about the ability to transfer assets held inside of Superannuation into tax-free environments before selling, they could have avoided every cent of tax payable.

As soon as you 'flick the switch' on the Superannuation tax structure from 'accumulation' to 'pension', every asset immediately becomes tax-free[87].

3B. TAX ON EARNINGS DROP TO 0%

For the entire wealth creation journey inside of Superannuation, you only pay 15% tax on all earnings by investments. And it gets even better from there. Once you hit pension phase, the tax then becomes 0%.

From the moment you start receiving income from your assets, your investment portfolio will live in an entirely tax-free environment, never to pay tax on investment earnings again.

3C. INCOME FROM SUPERANNUATION IS TAXED AT 0%

And finally the last benefit of reaching pension phase and having your assets inside of a Superannuation tax structure, is the income you draw down to fund your ideal lifestyle

87 / This is only possible with Wraps and SMSFs. Industry and Retail super funds hold assets on behalf of their members through Master Trusts, and cannot provide this.

when you no longer work is taxed at 0% also[88].

From the benefits above, you can see the Superannuation tax structure is the best entity for you to build an investment portfolio in the short term as you pay less tax today, the medium term as you pay less tax every year, and the long term when all assets and income become tax-free.

Now consider the only 'downside' of using Superannuation to build an investment portfolio: you can't spend the funds until you reach retirement. As I've continuously mentioned, an investment portfolio's purpose is only to be spent when you retire so I still have no qualms in putting forward the merits of Superannuation.

By having an external force such as salary sacrifice organised by your employment to make this decision for you, you are again outsourcing your financial decisions and reducing decision fatigue.

TYPES OF SUPER FUNDS

As you now have more insight into Superannuation than the majority of Australians, let's go through the four main types of Superannuation funds. These are governed by the same legislation but are priced differently based on the levels of flexibility and complexity.

---

88 / Only after age 60. From age 55 – 60 the income is taxed Marginal Tax Rates less 15%. This age 55 access is only available to those born before 1 July 1960. Sounds complicated but it isn't. If you are under age 50 now, you have to wait until you're 60.

INDUSTRY FUNDS

Let's start with the simplest, cheapest, and least flexible type of super fund, the Industry Super Fund. Industry Super have chosen to market themselves towards the 'typical Aussie battler', however they are just like every other type of financial institution. They want to manage as much money as possible to earn revenue.

Industry Super Funds were the first type of super funds in existence. Early on, you were given a hospitality Super Fund if you worked in hospitality and a construction Super Fund if you worked in construction. This has now changed, and anyone can open an Industry Super Fund.

Their typical client has low balances and lower understanding or interest in financial matters. Therefore an annual report from an Industry Super Fund will look something like this:

PRODUCT NAME	•Industry Super Fund A
INVESTMENT	•100% — Industry Super Fund A Balanced Fund
BALANCE	•$50,000
FEES	•Low — 0.50%

Industry Super Funds market themselves as non-profit entities benefiting the member. While that is a nice thing to say, Industry Funds earn big money, and I'm still yet to see a distribution paid back out to 'benefit the member'.

ADVANTAGES:
- You will probably already have one.
- They are the lowest cost in the market.
- Very simple investment options if your

financial literacy and interest are low.

DISADVANTAGES:
- Investment options are typically limited to investments branded the same name as the fund itself which are hard to research.
- No transparency on insurance payout figures.
- Don't directly own the assets.
- Do not have much flexibility.

RETAIL FUND

The second type of Superannuation fund is a Retail fund[89]. This type of Superannuation fund is almost identical to an Industry Super Fund, except owned by a big publically owned financial institution you would be familiar with.

The difference here is you have a little more flexibility in your investment choice outside of the house branded investments. For this additional flexibility, the price is generally a little higher than Industry Funds. A typical statement could look like this:

PRODUCT NAME	•Retail Super Fund
INVESTMENT	•1 Managed Fund 50% •2 Managed Fund 50%
BALANCE	•$100,000
FEES	•Low to Medium — 0.50% - 1%

89 / Another horrible name yet again providing absolutely no insight. A retail fund? Shouldn't a 'retail fund' be any fund available to a retail client? Yes, but where is the fun in finance if we aren't constantly confusing everyone!

ADVANTAGES:
- You will probably already have one
- They are relatively cost competitive
- A couple of investment options to choose from
- Transparency on insurance payout figures

DISADVANTAGES:
- Don't directly own the assets
- Do not have much flexibility

The third option in this confusing circus of Superannuation types is something called a Wrap. Now, if you have a Wrap, either you have a keen interest in financial literacy, or you have a Financial Adviser. These types of superannuation funds need to be specifically applied for.

Wraps allow holding a wider and more diverse list of managed funds, exchange traded funds (ETFs)[90] and direct equities, which allows a very specific investment strategy. They also allow you to hold the investments directly, creating the interesting scenario where the government pays you tax on fully franked dividends.

PRODUCT NAME	• Wrap
INVESTMENT	• 1 ETF — 20% • 2 ETF — 10% • 1 Managed Fund — 20% • 2 Managed Fund — 30% • 1 Australian Equity —10% • 2 Australian Equity —10%

90 / Some Industry and retail super funds offer ETFs and direct equities, but they aren't owned directly by the investor, the assets are owned by the fund's Master Trust. As such the tax benefits such as rebates on franked dividends, and the ability to move assets from accumulation to pension phase without paying any CGT do not exist.

BALANCE	•$300,000
FEES	•Medium to High — 1% - 1.5%

ADVANTAGES:
- Directly own assets for additional tax benefits
- Large investment selection

DISADVANTAGES:
- Need medium levels of financial literacy
- The costs are more expensive to match the flexibility.

SELF MANAGED SUPER FUNDS (SMSF)

The final option for your super fund is a Self Managed Super Fund (SMSF). Where there is confusion, people are naturally drawn to more control. As super is very hard to understand, the popularity of SMSFs has exploded over the last couple of years.

The issue is, SMSFs are easily the best option for those who know what they are doing, but the worst for those who don't. By that I mean, an SMSF has ultimate flexibility to invest in anything under super legislation, yet most people use it for very simple investments.

Facts are, unless you are holding fine art, real estate, gold bullion or complex financial instruments such as options within your super, there is zero point to owning an SMSF. And breathtakingly, less than 20% of SMSF assets are holding these types of assets.[91]

91 / www.superguide.com.au/smsfs/smsf-investment-diy-super-asset-types

From an emotional perspective, I understand why people want control of their super via an SMSF, but from a rational point of view, the large portion of assets held in managed funds, shares and cash, can all be held in far simpler and cheaper superannuation types.

SMSFs are the most difficult to run, and the most expensive to maintain. Accountants are required to set it up and maintain complex functions most people could not perform by themselves, which comes with a high cost.

While they do give you by far the most flexibility to invest in anything you want under superannuation law[92], unless you're using it to its best ability, you're driving a Ferrari down the street to drive-thru McDonalds.

PRODUCT NAME	•SMSF
INVESTMENT	•Commercial Real Estate 50% •Term Deposit 20% •1 ETF — 10% •2 ETF — 10% •1 Australian Equity — 5% •2 Australian Equity — 5%
BALANCE	•$1,000,000
FEES	•High — $3,000 Accountant fee P.A. •+1% for Investments

ADVANTAGES: • Directly own assets for additional tax benefits

92 / Superannuation Industry Supervision Act (SIS act). Another horrible name.

- Own any investment possible under Superannuation legislation

DISADVANTAGES:
- Need high levels of financial literacy
- Investor can get themselves into a lot of trouble
- Highest fees payable
- Complex laws that require ongoing assistance
- Can take a lot of time to manage correctly

CHAPTER SUMMARY

....

Q *How this helps fund your ideal lifestyle?*

Superannuation is purposefully boring and hard to understand, but don't let it sit in the 'too hard basket'. Once you get your head around this 'offshore bank account', you won't have to keep thinking about it, but you will benefit from it every year.

Building a portfolio of assets to fund your ideal lifestyle when you no longer work is best achieved through the tax advantages of superannuation. It has three main benefits. Firstly it will save you tax today by letting you keep the money and claim a tax deduction via something called 'salary sacrifice' (as opposed to negative gearing which requires you to lose the money to claim a tax deduction). Secondly your investment portfolio will benefit from a reduced tax rate every single year, and thirdly you can save a fortune by converting the assets to a 0% tax environment once you hit age 60 (or 55 if born before 1 July 1960)

All these tax benefits build up over the course of your wealth building to provide you with a far superior result. There is a reason the government has limits to how much you can deposit in each year. Once you understand the benefits, why would you build an investment portfolio any other way?

Q *How to make this easy?*

· Your employer handles salary sacrifice, and payroll calculates the immediate tax benefits. Therefore, after you have figured out how much you want to filter across to Superannuation via the calculator[93][94], this can be completely outsourced to automation.

---

93 / Don't overshoot the government limits. The limits include your mandatory employer Superannuation contributions, so you can only salary sacrifice the difference between how much you receive from your employer and the yearly Concessional Contribution Cap. These limits change every year but are easy to find if you know how to Google 'concessional contribution cap'. Talk to a Financial Adviser if you get lost.

94 / www.fundyourideallifestyle.com.au/calculator

Concourse A ↑
Ⓟ Terminal
Luggage Claim
🛃 Hotel

FOURTEEN

GO HARD OR GO HOME

INVESTING OFF THE BEATEN TRACK

"FORTUNE FAVOURS THE BOLD."

- AN OLD LATIN PROVERB

················ ✈ ················

"THERE'S A TREMENDOUS BIAS AGAINST TAKING RISKS.
EVERYONE IS TRYING TO OPTIMIZE THEIR ASS-COVERING."

- ELON MUSK

To this day I still remember being a tiny buck and having an absolute ball. Growing up with a single mum who hadn't decided yet to put her roots down anywhere meant we travelled a lot and lived amongst a broad community of friends and family over the course of a few years.

Most of my mum's friends had kids as well, so I'd have a bunch of new friends who were normally a little older than me to hang out with, and more than likely a bunch of 'new' hand-me-downs. I loved growing up in that setting, and I especially liked the hand-me-downs.

Can you imagine how happy I was to get my hands on things that were once owned by the 'older guys'? Whether t-shirts, shorts, or a basketball, I always had a story to accompany everything I owned.

It was never just a 'new' shirt. It was Nathan's or Shane's or Greg's shirt. And of course, being the little guy, I would always look up to these older boys and see how awesome they were at sports, and I wanted to be just like them.

So when a chest of draws covered in stickers ended up in my room at age eight after one of mum's friend's son had moved out of home to chase big wave riding around the world, I couldn't help but be enamoured with the motivational smorgasbord I got to look over every night.

These tiny billboards rewiring my pre-pubescent brain proudly promoted a nonchalant view of self-preservation and read phrases like 'No Guts, No Glory, Go For it', and 'Go Hard or Go Home'.

It made perfect sense considering his penchant for riding on large masses of moving ocean water, but to me, it was an insight into how to be more like those grown up boys I'd spent my whole childhood admiring.

And as these stickers casually embedded themselves into my psyche over the course of the next decade, the overarching simplicity started to appeal to me. The message was, don't let fear hold you back, you can have anything you want.

I am very aware for a subset of the population, the idea of passively sitting by to build a safe and secure diversified investment in a tax efficient environment is going to be too boring. Despite putting forward the proven way to build an investment portfolio with tax efficiencies and little ongoing decision making, some will still want to pursue high-octane investments.

So I've written this chapter to give some boundaries to those with the hubris to think they can beat the long odds and make it in the perilous field of high risk investing.

Not only does this type of investing lead to a high probability of losses, but the time and effort involved in getting to the point of mastery here will be a long-term drain on your time, money and cognitive minimalism.

With all that said, it's now time to pull the handbrake like a Matrix II-style car pileup, and go hard or go home. If you are determined to build a portfolio with high-risk investments, I'm going to give you every chance possible to come out the other side alive.

If you want to be more involved with your investments, it's going to be through a lot of research, a lot of hard work, and limiting the exposure of your investment portfolio to downsides. If things go bad, you reduce the fallout, and if things go well, you shouldn't need more than a small percentage of your investment portfolio to reap the rewards.

My goal in this chapter is to inform you of the risks and benefits of high-risk investing, and if you insist on doing so, giving you a framework to achieve it. In my opinion, investing shouldn't be sexy, but I will provide a realistic view of how much study, work, and time it takes to master. Just know that, even then, the odds are stacked against you.

THE SOPHISTICATED ANGEL

Out of all the laws designed to protect people from themselves, I'd say the restriction to stop people from accessing the most profitable deals on offer takes the cake. It all comes down to whether you qualify as a 'sophisticated investor' or not.

If your income or assets reach the threshold[95], the government lets you through the ropes and onto the court to the big league to invest in startups by way of Angel investing. The thinking is, at this stage, you know what you're doing with your money so you don't need protection from yourself any longer.

If you don't hit these requirements, you are considered a 'retail investor' and not allowed to partake in startup investments. The reason? Well, the government doesn't think you have enough money, so it doesn't give you the chance to make more money. So for those that are over this threshold, congratulations, you have the ability to become an Angel investor.

95 / The threshold at time of writing is $250,000 annual income, or $2.5M net assets.

Here's the good, the bad, and the ugly.

The good news is Angel investing is making the best investors exceedingly wealthy. If you spend an hour on angel.co, you can see the portfolios built up by some of the Angels on there.

The bad news is even if you think investing in startups is a casual fun activity, there is a mountain of bad offers to filter through before getting to the good ones. And once you invest your money, you won't be outsourcing this to automation and benefiting from cognitive minimalism to get better results in other areas of your life. No way. You're going to be doing whatever you can to help them succeed. Angel investing is investing more than just your money; it's investing your time.

Hence why you should only focus on industries with which you already have some familiarity. If you're an Angel investor, you're going to double as an adviser. You'll be so close to the company, and given that your money is tied to the precarious journey, you'll do whatever you can to help it succeed.

If you don't take this advice and end up investing in fluorescent miniature submarines, don't be surprised when you're spending twenty hours a week researching government rulings on underwater sea craft, anti-terrorism laws, and how best to send bulk packages to Russia incognito.

Finally, you require a well-connected network of other Angel investors. The truth is, the best investments get identified early, and go from being obscure to oversubscribed overnight. Your ability to get in early on the best deals will depend almost entirely on whom you know.

GIVE YOURSELF OPTIONS

If you come under the threshold and still want to roll the dice with high-risk investments, you can substitute Angel investing with another avenue of exponential growth: leverage.

Leverage is very common. In fact, the size of the derivative market is many times larger than the global money supply[96]. And the easiest way to access leverage is through, trading options.

Options did take me a little while to understand when I first started researching them. However once I had my head around the concept, I created a little table which makes things far easier to understand.

BUY *The Right* TO BUY	BUY *The Right* TO SELL
SELL *The Right* TO BUY	SELL *The Right* TO SELL

Top line big picture, as you can see you either 'buy' an option or 'sell' an option. Just like a can of Coke. One person buys, one person sells. As the 'buyer', you can buy one of two different products. You can buy 'the right to buy', or you can buy 'the right to sell'.

96 / Great visualisation http://money.visualcapitalist.com/all-of-the-worlds-money-and-markets-in-one-visualization/

Buying 'the right to buy' means you pay a small amount of money in exchange 'for the right' to buy an equity at a certain price. For example, if Apple shares are currently $1 and you think the price will go to $2, then instead of buying the Apple stock outright, you instead pay a smaller amount to buy 'the right' to purchase Apple at $1.

As you pay a smaller amount for 'the right' to buy Apple at $1, you can purchase 100x more. Then, when Apple goes up to $2, you execute 'the right' to buy Apple at $1, and sell for $2 immediately. Using the same level of investment, you were able to increase your profit 100x by using options rather than buying Apple stock outright.

Sounds good, doesn't it? Of course, in reality, it is rather hard to figure out if Apple is going to $2 in the first place. On the other side, if Apple never moved from $1, and you never had the chance to execute 'the right' to buy, then the amount you paid would be a loss to you, and seen as income to the investor who sold you 'the right' to buy in the first place.

Which brings me to the 'sell' side of an options trade. Buying an option requires someone to be the seller. In exchange for a small amount of money, the seller sells you 'the right' to buy. For example, the seller of the Option believes Apple will not go up in value, as such the investor sells you 'the right' to buy in exchange for some money. If the share stays where it is, you don't execute the trade and the seller keeps the money. If Apple does go up in value, the seller is obligated to sell you their Apple stock for $1, which you sell for $2 and make money.

As the buyer, the second product you can purchase is 'the right' to sell Apple at $1 if you think it is going down in value. In this example, you buy 'the right' to sell Apple at $1, and then Apple stock plummets to 50 cents. At this stage, you execute the trade and immediately buy Apple at 50 cents, and sell it for $1. As in the previous example, because you used options, you were able to leverage your position and increase your earning by 100x.

The seller of the option sold you 'the obligation' to buy the Apple stock at $1, and as Apple is now only worth 50 cents, the seller of this Option is obligated to buy at $1, and sell back to the market at 50 cents. In other words, they lost a lot of money. If Apple stock had stayed at $1, then the investor would have kept the money you paid to buy 'the right' to sell as income.

The amount of money at risk when you 'buy the right' to either buy or sell is limited to the cost of the Option. As such, you know how much you are set to lose if your assumption is wrong. The good news is your upside is only limited to how correct you were in your assumption if the stock moves in the direction you wanted. Small downside risk, high upside.

Where things can go horribly wrong, is when you 'sell the obligation'. Once you start selling the obligation to either buy or sell, you are opening yourself up to pandemonium. In the same way as your upside potential is unlimited when you 'buy the right', your downside risk is unlimited when you 'sell the obligation'[97].

---

97 / Option traders do regularly 'sell the obligation', however they use other trades to 'hedge' their bets

ASSUME YOU WILL LOSE

The best starting block you can build from is the assumption you will lose. The stats on successful Angel investing and options trading is dismal. So by drowning out your enthusiasm, your chances to start making investment decisions based on due diligence increase.

High-risk investments need a thorough investment philosophy. While 'time and diversification' work for stable investments, high-risk investments require a considerable amount of due diligence.

Startups are judged on the management team's history of executing, the potential profitability of the idea, the size of the market, and the ease at which you can provide the service or product to the market. It's a lot more than 'my friend has a great business idea'.

Options trades are judged on technical analysis like daily averages, fundamental research and intrinsic value, reading up on all the news releases, and being willing to bet against billion dollar super computers. It isn't 'I have a hot tip from a friend'.

With all this in mind, you still have to assume you will lose. Angel investing means taking a small group of entrepreneurs with no systems or internal policies from conception to execution to success. It's a hard task. In fact, the chances of it becoming a unicorn[98] are less than one in a thousand of the ventures which are considered successful.

And perfectly reading the technical data to support an options trade can be offset by an obscure news report, a shift in currency,

---

98 / A unicorn is a company that ends up being worth over a billion dollars. Called as such for how rare they are.

or a government policy change. With so many moving parts, it's hard to know what data to rely on.

High-risk investing is not something you can do well 'part time' and requires a time commitment to master. And even with this kind of respect, at the end of the day, it's as close to gambling as possible.

Most VC firms do not make much money. The proprietary knowledge handed down over many years by the top 20% of Venture Capital firms explains why they make 80% of all the money. If the top VC firms struggle, what are the chances of someone walking in as an Angel investor and cleaning up?

And the vast majority of day traders do not make any money[99]. Again, if those who trade frequently struggle, what are the chances of someone picking it up part time and succeeding?

Hopefully, you can see this is not easy money. If you choose to invest in high-risk investments regardless, you will have to focus on improving your investment intelligence and your ability to deal well with pressure to build a systematic way of managing the high-risk.

THE TALEB-DALIO PORTFOLIO

The best place to start with managing this type of risk is to decide how much exposure your investment portfolio should have to high-risk investments. In answering, I step aside to the experi-

---

99 / Barber, Lee, Odeon, Liu (2010): *Do Day Traders Rationally Learn About Their Ability?*

ence and results of two of the world's greatest investment minds, Nassim Taleb and Ray Dalio.

To start with I'd like to introduce you to an investment theory called the 'Barbell Strategy' popularized by Nassim Taleb's 2007 book *The Black Swan*.

This investment philosophy is predicated on the fact that a diversified portfolio isn't set up to earn massive results, and trying to do so only opens you up to greater chances of loss for a minimal chance at higher gains.

> *"If you know you're vulnerable to prediction errors,*
> *and accept most 'risk measures' are flawed, your strategy is to*
> *be as hyper-conservative and hyper-aggressive as you can be,*
> *instead of being mildly aggressive or conservative."*

- NASSIM TALEB

Like the barbell thrown around by beasts in a gym, the Barbell Strategy[100] states to have small weights on the furthest edge of each side of the portfolio, with the bulk of the weight centred in the middle.

---

100 / There are a few iterations of the barbell theory. Taleb himself prefers to make no money from the safe majority of the portfolio and invest 85% of his money in Bonds. His intention is for this portion of his investment portfolio to survive in a worst-case scenario, and to make money solely from his high-risk investments. I will also note he says to make money with businesses instead of options trading as it takes years to get good, and again, no guarantee.

The two smaller weights on the ends of the barbell represent the extremes in the portfolio. On one extreme you invest in the safest option possible and on the other extreme high-risk. In this case, cash on one side, and startups or options on the other.

Essentially, you are offsetting the risks attached to each type of investment. The risk of losing all your money on the high-risk side, coupled with the security your money not moving at all on the other side. Leaving the bulk of your money in the middle in a diversified portfolio. Here it is:

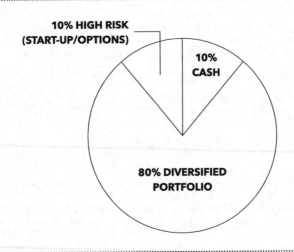

Taleb's point is that you're better off being safe with the bulk of your money, and taking a small amount and trying to hit a home run with it.

To decide what the greater part of the portfolio could look like, I'll introduce Ray Dalio's 'All Weather Portfolio' made popular in Tony Robbins book *Money Master the Game: 7 Simple Steps to Financial Freedom*.

The point of Dalio's All-Weather strategy is similar to the bulk of Taleb's portfolio. No one has a crystal ball, so it makes sense to prepare for anything – inflation, deflation, rising economic growth or slowing economic growth. If the top hedge fund manager in the world admits to the impossibility of predicting the economic outlook, what luck do the rest of us have?

In simplistic investing terms, it is a bond-heavy portfolio. What I like about it, though, is the diversification to alternatives, with gold and commodities both getting a look in. Here it is:

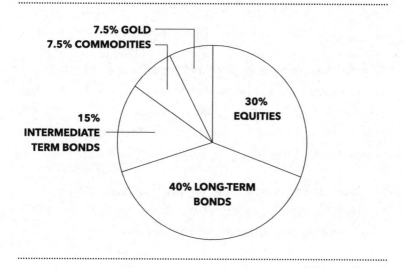

Combining both these investment philosophies brings us to the Taleb-Dalio portfolio. Using the Barbell Theory, we put 10% to the extremes of cash and high-risk, with the All Weather portfolio making up the bulk of the weight with an 80% diversified portfolio.

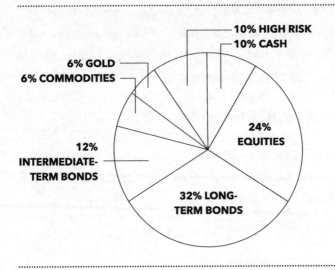

With the 10% of your money you have allocated to high-risk, if you are a sophisticated investor and choose to invest in startups, you should look to invest across ten investments. This reduces your exposure to any particular high-risk investment to only 1% of your total net worth.

If you are trading options, split the allocated amount up in to one hundred amounts allowing for 0.1% of your total net worth. This gives you room to learn and improve over time.

If you spread your high-risk investments thinly enough, you won't need to rely on, or be overly emotionally involved in any particular investment. If you decide to pursue high-risk invest-ments, the Taleb-Dalio portfolio gives you the positive restraints needed to stay in the game for as long as possible, and give you the time to create success.

WORK FOR OPTIONS

If you're not interested in ruining your cognitive minimalism learning about Angel investing or trading options, and if you like the potential of high-risk investments but don't want to risk your capital, you still have the possibility of working for a startup. This strategy allows you to receive a salary, keep focusing on your professional skill set, all the while getting your hands on some options.

Working for options is a safe way to invest in high-risk investments with the additional benefit of not needing to satisfy the sophisticated investor rules. Some startups offer options as a part of the remuneration strategy, and others require you to buy-in. Either way, as an integral part of the success of the company, you can have a positive effect on the outcome. In a way, you reduce the investment risk with your blood, sweat, and tears.

Also, working in a startup will teach you over time what it takes to get a successful venture off the ground. If you spent a couple of years building a small company with a team of people, how capable would you be at gauging whether another startup had the ability to succeed?

I'd say you'd be a lot more confident in your ability to tell if a particular idea has the potential of a positive outcome. In turn, this builds the skills needed to be a successful Angel investor. The only downside to working for options is you won't be building a diversified portfolio of startups.

And finally, if you do end up working for a startup that becomes successful, you can end up with multiple times your salary with the profits from the shares.

If you want to get into the startup market without risking your money, then working for options is a great compromise.

CHAPTER SUMMARY

....

Q *How this helps fund your ideal lifestyle?*

The purpose of building an investment portfolio is to provide yourself with an income later in life when you no longer work. The more valuable your investment portfolio is when you reach this point, the higher your ongoing income.

While building a diversified portfolio is the best low-touch way to achieve this, some people want to wade into the murky world of high-risk investments. If this is you, know up front you are up against the odds.

With that said, if you are so inclined to dip your toe in the water of high-risk, high-touch, and high-potential investments, startups and trading options are your best bet.

Q *How to make this easy?*

This one is hard, as you can't make investing in startups or trading options simple. It's going to take study, experience, and networking to excel in this type of investing.

If you choose to pursue high-risk investments, then use the Taleb-Dalio portfolio. Keep 10% in cash, 80% in a diversified portfolio, and only allocate 10% of your investment portfolio towards high-risk investments.

If you're putting the 10% allocated to high-risk investing into startups, spread this risk among ten investments. Doing so reduces your exposure to 1% of your total investment portfolio to each investment.

If you are trading options, spread the 10% across one hundred trades and reduce your exposure to 0.1% of your total investment portfolio to each individual investment.

For startups, read books such as *The Lean Startup* by Eric Ries and *Venture Deals* by Brad Feld and Jason Mendelson. Most importantly, stick to startups in fields where you have professional experience. You don't want to be constantly running around researching information to help; you want to be talking from experience.

If you don't quite hit the barriers to entry to be an accredited investor and instead focus on options trading, the same rules apply. Best books to read here are *The Bible of Options Strategies* by Guy Cohen and *The Market Guys' Five Points for Trading Success* by A J Monte and Rick Swope.

If you really want to make investing easy, don't invest in these types of assets at all. An ideal outcome after reading this chapter would be to say, 'Nope, too hard for me', and avoid startup investing or options trading altogether.

FIFTEEN

START SMALL, GET SCREWED

ENTREPRENEURS ADD ZEROS

"MY INTEREST IN LIFE COMES FROM SETTING MYSELF
HUGE, APPARENTLY UNACHIEVABLE CHALLENGES
AND TRYING TO RISE ABOVE THEM."

- RICHARD BRANSON

"NOBODY COUNTS YOUR FAILURES,
YOU JUST HAVE TO BE RIGHT ONCE."

- MARK CUBAN

At twenty-one years of age, I realised I was an entrepreneur. Having just come down from a six-year creative high playing music, the first time I heard about being paid handsomely for solving problems and creating new things for the world, I immediately knew it was for me.

And like some Viking Berserker, I started solving problems. Many problems. Any problem. In fact, I wandered into any area I thought could benefit from my view of a better world. Needless to say, I had no idea of what I was doing and ended up in areas I had no business being in.

For example, I decided toilet seats should be easier to use. So I built some plans for a new type of toilet seat. It started out as a push pedal similar to a rubbish bin (still a superb idea), then morphed into a state of the art piece of technology, sliding back horizontally into the wall to steam clean itself after use.

Voila, I thought, everyone is going to love this. I jumped in the car, drove a couple of hours to have a meeting with someone specialising in patents, sat down, and told them my idea. From here I thought it was just a matter of cashing cheques.

However, something happened that I wasn't prepared for. The patent guy wasn't particularly impressed with my idea. He instead pulled out a little contraption that spun lollipops inside people's mouths and explained it was the most successful item his office had ever produced to date. He said its success came from its simplicity. And he said my idea was not simple.

'Fair enough' I thought. He had me there. The idea was not particularly simple. And while I didn't want to be known for creating lollipop spinners, I supposed I didn't want to be known as 'the toilet guy' either and dumped[101] the idea shortly after.

Then I moved on to my next idea, MovieMe. A decade before I had heard of Netflix, I put together a business plan to stream movies directly to a computer.

I spent a couple of months building a business plan with statistics around the decline of the video store, and how the rise of internet speeds could facilitate a new way of delivering movies. I pitched my idea, and these were the three questions I got asked:

A   *Is this a university project?*

B   *How old are you?*

C   *What do you know about the movie industry?*

I think the fact I had spent more time on the logo than anything else in the document, was only just twenty-two years old and knew nothing about the movie industry other than 'I like movies' was more than enough reason to pass up on the seed round of my startup[102].

With my inability to convince those who actually understood how the business worked, I figured I'd finally attempt something simple. So, I looked around my house, picked up a pair of boxers and decided to start a men's underwear business.

---

101 / Pun? Yes. Intended.

102 / Actually, it gets worse. To be honest, I didn't even realise I was there to pitch for capital. With zero understanding of next steps, or what it takes to build a company, I didn't even know I was pitching for money. I can't quite remember what I thought was going to happen, I assume I just thought I would put forward the idea and like magic it would be implemented and I would be rich because it was such a good idea. So, so, so, so, so, so, so bad.

Because edgy is always a good starting point, I decided to call the boxer company 'Man Holder' because, you know, it's edgy. First things first I decided I needed a buyer. On a big scale. So I called up Target.

Target is a big company, and with no direct number to call the people who make the decisions I started with the next best option. I opened the Yellow Pages and called my local Target. Within two minutes I was speaking with the national merchandiser for men's underwear, and we organised a showcase[103].

At this point, he mentioned that if he was happy with my stock, I had to be able to provide five hundred thousand pairs within ninety days. I said I would come back to him to see if my manufacturing could handle it, he gave me his email, and I hung up the phone.

I had no business, no product, not even a logo. In fact, I didn't even know what a showcase was, but I started making calls. I called around and found some Chinese manufacturers who could deliver half a million pairs of boxers in ninety days for the small price of one hundred thousand dollars.

And despite how much fun I had in that one afternoon putting together a business idea and creating myself an opportunity out of nothing, I chickened out. In hindsight, I responsibly decided the prospect of finding and spending a hundred thousand dollars with-

---

103 / This is a ridiculous story. I called my local Target, who put me through to the state merchandiser, who put me through to the national merchandiser. Within two minutes of making a call to a local outlet, I was speaking to the guy who decides nation-wide what brand of men's underwear the sell. I learned how to do this by talking to people who had successfully snuck backstage when I was playing shows. It was always the same response — just walk as if you have to be somewhere quickly and no one will stop you. Turns out it works with phone calls too.

out a guarantee I could sell them was not exactly smart business.

I'm sharing these embarrassing moments so you understand that from the moment I heard the word 'entrepreneur', I wanted to be one. If I didn't create music for people any longer, I was going to create products and services. And even though I knew less than nothing about how to get there, I knew I was going to do it. Similarly, if you know absolutely nothing, but want to as well, then I have no reason to doubt it.

The good news all this time spent haphazardly trying to be an entrepreneur wasn't for nothing. After coming up with these (and many more) scatter brain ideas, I realised there are really only three questions which need answering to know if an idea is going to be successful or not:

Will this improve lives by solving a genuine problem people are experiencing at scale, or is it just a 'good idea'?

Does this idea come from a unique insight provided by someone experienced in the field?

Does the team have the ability (ideally the history) of executing and implementing?

As you have joined me on this adventure so far, stay with me in this final chapter. I've included entrepreneurship in this book because a) I love it, so it was always going to turn up, b) it's the riskiest kind of investing (not just towards your money, but also your time, your reputation, and your career progression), and c) it's the safest and surest way to make real money.

Investing doesn't make much money. Again, it's fine over the long term, but pretty useless in the short term and high-risk investing is a long shot against the odds. Being an entrepreneur, on the other hand, can help build more money in the short term than an investment, and a much higher chance of success than Angel investing or options trading.

GET AN MBA IN YOUR CLIENT'S PROBLEMS

To ensure you are providing a complete and remarkable solution to an actual problem, you first have to decide who is your ideal client, and what problem you are going to solve for them. Then you need to prove you understand their problem better than they do themselves. Put simply: you need an MBA in your client's problems.

If you can articulate to your ideal market the problems they face, why they face them, and what they can do to fix them, you will be seen as an expert. The go-to they call when they're ready to make a change.

To that end here are a couple of exercises to complete. Regardless of whether you currently have a business, are looking to start one, or want additional insights for your job, it will be worth your time to complete these thoroughly.

.... EXERCISE 15.1 ....

Identify five to ten people as a sample of your ideal market and ask these questions:
....

Q   *What would you say are your 3 top problems?*
....

_____

_____

_____

....

Q *What stresses you out?*

....

_____

_____

_____

_____

....

Q *If you could just have a break from something, what would that be?*

....

_____

_____

_____

Q   *If you find yourself worrying, what is it about?*

_____

_____

_____

_____

Q   *If you could fix one thing in your life/business what would that be?*

_____

_____

_____

_____

Q   *What do you wish you had more of?*

_____

_____

_____

_____

Q *What do you wish you had less of?*

Q *As you think about where you would like to be in life/business, what's currently stopping you?*

Q *If funding wasn't a problem, what would be the first thing you would invest in for your business/life?*

EXERCISE 15.2

Using the answers from the questions above and your existing insights into this target market, write down one hundred problems your ideal client will likely experience on a day-to-day basis.

I know this can be rather daunting, but for the hour or so of pain you go through to come up with these, you will build the foundations of your business.

_____

_____

_____

EXERCISE 15.3

Once you have one hundred problems, you should be able to distill these down to seven key areas. These seven key areas you should learn off by heart. They will act as the backbone of all your messages moving forward in blogs, articles, podcasts, etc.

1 _____

2 _____

3 _____

4 _____

5 _____

6 _____

7 _____

·················· **EXERCISE 15.4** ··················

Now you have your seven top problems, distill these further down to three key problems. These main three issues will be in all your marketing, and your goal will be to become known as the expert in these three problems.

These problems will also be what your business aims to solve. Whether you can personally solve the entire problem by yourself is irrelevant. You can always get other experts in to fill the gaps. But your company has to be known as the go-to for these three areas.

1 _____

_____

2 _____

_____

3 _____

_____

··············· EXERCISE 15.5 ···············

Finally distill these three problems down to one key and central problem. If you can articulate in one sentence, every problem your ideal market is experiencing, especially in a way they have never heard before, then you will immediately be seen as the expert in helping to solve that problem.

KEY AND CENTRAL PROBLEM:

_____

_____

_____

_____

_____

ADDING ZEROS

Once you have identified your market, and what problems you're going to solve, the next step is to give yourself quantitative points to hit. How much money should you aim to make? As with everything else, look to make it easy on yourself.

So maybe you can't make a million dollars straight away, but surely you can make a single dollar. By achieving a small goal early on, you can use this motivation to keep going. Being an entrepreneur requires optimism, may as well breed success from the start.

Making even a single dollar from business is not easy. You still need to identify a target market and an exact problem, and you still need to create a product or service to solve the problem. You then need to market the solution and deliver the solution.

Entrepreneurship is the process of finding out what the market wants, and giving it to them. And you are going to make endless mistakes refining this process. The lessons you learn from earning a dollar from the business will already reveal to you some mistakes you need to fix to make more.

Because once you make a single dollar, from there, it's a case of adding zeros. One dollar becomes ten; ten becomes one hundred. A thousand, then ten thousand. And with every zero you add, you learn new things to take you to the next zero.

Every zero you add brings a new level of problems to solve, and a new level of lessons learned to overcome those problems. Your entrepreneurial intelligence increases with every zero. It's fine to be making rookie mistakes at ten dollars, but not at a million.

The biggest and most obvious mistakes you make while your business is small is a good thing. You want all the major growing pains and obvious mistakes out of the way before anyone really notices what you're doing.

With each zero you add to the top line, you will learn better systems, and better ways of doing business. You'll also get a better reputation. The people who can help you progress in your career as an entrepreneur, let's call them the Gatekeepers, generally only let those in who have tried. If you're trying to succeed and someone can see that, your chances of getting a hand up increase a hundred fold.

No one wants to give assistance to someone who won't appreciate it or take advantage of it. Every mentor wants someone who has the potential to be successful. By proving you are trying, even if you are failing and making mistakes, you will gain the attention of the people you want.

If you want a mentor who brings in a million dollars a year, they will only be interested in spending their time helping you if you have already gone through the lessons learned from one dollar up to one hundred thousand dollars. By simply starting a business and adding zeros, you are showing the Gatekeepers you are worth their time.

And it's not just mentors who decide how much time they are willing to spend on you based on your prior work. Angel investors and venture capitalists will want to know your progress. Even banks these days judge you on your entrepreneurial story.

If you turn up with 'an idea', you will be laughed out of the office, but if you can show progressive sales results, building a small business into one turning over ten million dollars a year, you are going to get let through a lot of locked doors.

Starting small and adding a zero is by far and away the best way I've found to build a company up from nothing while building your experience, your reputation, and your ability to access mentors and get through the Gatekeepers.

THE PERFECTIONIST PARADOX

I've found a lot of very capable people suffer from something I call the perfectionist paradox. It's proven to be the final hurdle before someone backs themselves to start on the journey to becoming an entrepreneur.

First, let me explain. Your mind is a thinking machine. That's what it does, that's what it's meant to do, that is its purpose. However, nothing in the user manual suggests your thoughts have to benefit you. A thriving psychology industry is proof of this.

And over the course of many years, I noticed two common thought patterns in high achieving and high performing people who had the makings of an entrepreneur, but never took the step: a) they were often perfectionists, and b) oddly enough they also had a self-sabotaging streak.

On the surface, it seemed like a contradiction. How could one hold these two opposing thoughts? But it occurred to me one day, as one afflicted by this limiting behaviour, that self-sabotaging is an inbuilt safety mechanism for the perfectionist.

See, a perfectionist can't accept mistakes or failure (it's inherent in being a perfectionist). And the hardest thing for a perfectionist to do is to look into a mirror and admit they were the cause of failure.

So if something is getting tough, the perfectionist has two options. Either put the internal reputation as a perfectionist on the line by working hard to try to turn the problem around or, if the chances of success are low, unconsciously sabotage it.

Self-sabotaging gives room to hide behind a wall of self-deceit and avoid taking responsibility for the outcome. It preserves the myth of 'I can do anything' despite objective evidence to the contrary. Sure, it takes a special kind of mental gymnastics to get there, but as I mentioned above, the brain doesn't always work to the owner's benefit.

I mention this now because if you decide to start small, the final piece of the puzzle to solve is not to wait until everything is 'perfect' before moving ahead. You will make mistakes; you will experience failure. It doesn't matter. Start anyway.

If you want to start on the road to entrepreneurialism, don't let the potential for an unwanted outcome stop you from moving forward, even if you are a perfectionist. Get the bravado to start, and the gumption to look at yourself in the mirror and be responsible for the outcome of your efforts. Success or failure, it's on you. Own it.

COMPLETE & REMARKABLE SOLUTION

After spending the majority of the last few years with other entrepreneurs, I've discovered we fall into one of two categories. One brings me to life, and the other makes me want to punch myself in the face.

It's all centred on why someone is in business in the first place. Put simply, are they in business because they have figured out a unique way to solve problems by providing a complete and remarkable solution? Or is it just for the money?

Easy money is, unfortunately, easy to make. All it takes is a *Wolf of Wall Street* selling mentality. The problem we all have with sales is the fact that people can make something sound far better than what it is. We all hate being ripped off, and we all hate paying for something that comes in far below our expectations.[104]

Or is the goal of the entrepreneur to give people a remarkable solution, an outcome where the client experiences real change for the better and over the long term? Does the entrepreneur possess unique insights and experiences that can be distilled into a product or service to make the world a better place? Or is their skill set limited to being great at sales, and offering little in the way of value?

Being a successful entrepreneur leads to more money, and less time spent on the functioning day-to-day type of work. You can elevate yourself above being a cog in the wheel. As a result, being an entrepreneur is a pretty alluring possibility for a lot of people.

But what kind of entrepreneur are you going to be? There is nothing wrong with making a good profit, but is your goal about giving or taking? Do you want to be useful or greedy? Are you aiming to make the world a better place or are you only interested in banking cheques?

The money is there of course, but it is a reward, not a purpose. It is a scoreboard representing how accurately you provided what people wanted. It should not be the 'why' behind the business.

---

104 / The good news is that being good at sales doesn't predicate a bad client outcome, and being bad at sales doesn't predicate a good client outcome. This is why it's important to start with having a complete and remarkable solution. Once what you provide is world class, sending an army of salespeople out to sell it makes perfect sense.

Entrepreneurship is the best way I know to build wealth in the short term. So if you're already an entrepreneur or if you want to become one, do you want to bring value to other people's lives or are you only after a nicer car or fancier apartment? It won't make your journey any easier or harder, but it will make it infinitely more enjoyable.

CHAPTER SUMMARY

....

Q *How this helps fund your ideal lifestyle?*

This chapter is for the riskiest type of investing: starting your own company. It's not for everyone, but I included it because many people are beginning to think entrepreneurially, and it's the best way to build wealth in the short term.

Q *How to make this easy?*

The first step is to understand your ideal client's problems better than they do. If you can show mastery over the main concerns for a particular target market, and show them how to fix these problems, you will build up a level of trust that won't be overcome by any other type of advertising by competitors.

Start small. Don't put pressure on yourself to achieve everything straight away. Earn one dollar from business and keep building zeros on the end. You will learn lessons and make mistakes along the way with each level, ultimately building a solid base of entrepreneurial experience and knowledge.

Don't wait until you everything is perfect before you start. Having the tenacity to start a new project when things are still only 50% clear is completely normal. As you continue along the journey, things become clearer. And at all costs, keep that perfectionist paradox locked in its cage. Be willing to accept success or failure is on you.

Finally, build a complete and remarkable solution for your clients. This will ensure what you provide is first class. While business is the best way to build wealth in the short term, don't let that be your main focus. Ensure your focus is to create long-term positive change for everyone you work with.

EPILOGUE

YOUR IDEAL LIFESTYLE IS A JOURNEY
NOT A DESTINATION

A brief confession:

wrote this book after seeing the improvements in the lives of my clients and delving into it enough to create a replicable framework. And while I believe in everything I've written, I'm embarrassed by the audaciousness of the title.

Referring to an 'ideal lifestyle' makes it sound like I'm talking about a destination, an outcome or ending to reach. Follow these steps and life will be a breeze from this day forward. It sounds like a fairy tale.

But it isn't. It's a journey.

One that I'm still on.

And to fully pull the curtain aside, I want to share something most people in my professional circle would be surprised to hear. I've done my best over my career trying to avoid revealing it, but for the sake of proving how real the results of my system are I've decided to share it.

Here it is: even though I've dedicated my life to understanding and working with money, I still grapple with insecurity about it.

My family didn't have money while I was growing up. In my household, there was a lot of love, laughter, and fun – but not much by way of financial security or comfort. In fact, my early childhood was mostly spent travelling around living with friends and family or in public housing.

We were never destitute, my mother would never have allowed it, but we had to make do. And as a kid, I never knew we lived differently from anyone else, but over time that changed.

Growing up, my family figured out all kinds of ways to provide me with what I needed. For example when I lived with some extended family, my uncle worked at a fruit and vegetable shop and was able to bring home the stock that wasn't fit to sell.

Being young, I had no problem with the fact that the produce wasn't picture perfect. All I knew was that before I ate the apple, an adult had to 'cut the bad bit out'. Simple. Except it didn't translate too well when I went to a friend's birthday and wouldn't eat the apple I was given until the bad bit had been cut out.

There I was sitting in a group of children shocked at everyone's cavalier attitude of simply biting into a perfectly decent piece of fruit. I, on the other hand, took mine up to the responsible adult and asked them to 'cut the bad bit out'. After an awkward moment of silence, the fruit was handed back to me with a small piece removed. I was then happy to start eating.

And while that may seem outrageous, the funny part is my upbringing was not dramatically different from everyone else in my community. Sure, we ate unattractive fruit and vegetables[105], but

---

105 / That wasn't even the hard part. We also had goats. Those goats had milk. For the record, goat's milk should not be drunk.

everyone struggled. It was a small town on the east coast of Australia in the eighties – no one really had anything.

I couldn't stay insulated from the truth of my reality forever though. The older I got, the more aware I became.

That realisation hit me hard the first time I saw Sydney. I took a train down to the city to stay with my dad for the first time in my life. He had lived in Canada up until I was sixteen, and now that he had moved home it was time to catch up.

We walked into a café and I bought a coffee for the first time. To me, coffee was only something you make at home with hot water and a tea spoon of brown powder. Now I was looking at a coffee *menu*. All the different names – very few of which seemed to be written in English – were making my head spin.

As I looked down the list of the ten or so different types of coffees I couldn't identify a single one. *Cappuccino, latte, macchiato, espresso* – I wasn't Italian, I had no idea what they were.

Not wanting to seem like the small town boy I so clearly was, I ordered the cheapest item on the menu: espresso. I didn't want to be a financial burden to a bloke I had just met, and out of the list it was the only one I thought rang a bell. I had probably seen it in a movie or something.

When this tiny shot of coffee got placed in front of me, I tried to hide my surprise. The taste of it was stronger than anything I had experienced in my life, and I sat there, slowly sipping it for the better part of half an hour.

We later walked around Darling Harbour and I'll never forget how completely out of my depth I felt the entire time. There was an entire world where people who 'knew things' operated on a different level to where I grew up. I was surrounded by tall buildings, infinite Italian coffee choices... I couldn't help but wonder what else I didn't know, how far behind I might be. I sensed it was a lot.

I jumped on a train home and felt relieved as we pulled out of the station. I was going back to a place where coffee was coffee and a two-story house was a big deal. The only difference was now I knew what else was out there.

It may have felt good to come home, but my perspective was different now. I saw that I was different.

Fast forward a decade and I finally move to Sydney. I start applying for jobs and a recruiter scans my CV, notices I don't have any experience in Sydney and says, 'You know, Sydney has a competitive job market'. Without missing a beat I said, 'Then I feel sorry for the other applicants'. Even though I had come so far, I still had so much further to go.

I score a junior role in a brilliant company. Except, very quickly it became apparent I didn't fit in. At all. This was my first experience meeting people who had gone to 'the right' schools, and had parents who sat on boards of companies who could get them great jobs.

These were the type of people who scored in the top 10% nationwide for the end of high school marks. I had barely passed, having spent my senior high school years at the beach or in the recording studio[106].

As I had just moved to Sydney with no support network I had to pay six months rent upfront to secure accommodation, which all meant I could only afford the one suit[107].

Now in Nambucca Heads if you wear a suit – even at a wedding or funeral, you're going to get looks. But in Sydney, in the office I was in, if you wear the same suit more than twice a week people are going to start talking. How things had changed.

So again, I felt out of place. I did whatever I could to make the outfit look different. I scoured eBay and bought as many $5 cufflinks and ties as possible. But, as I'm sure you can guess, nothing worked.

In the end I was asked to leave. I understand why, companies have to foster a culture and I didn't fit it. This was an office full of people with the right backgrounds, and that wasn't me.

The funny thing is, having spent my entire adult life feeling like I didn't know enough or have enough to fit in, I've tried my absolute hardest over a long time to reach a point where I feel like I fit in both mentally and economically.

The good news is I've arrived at a point where I finally do feel adequate. The bad news is I'm prone to be overly opinionated, and I *still* find myself being frugal. I still have to remind myself repeat-

---

106 / The one benefit of living like a monk at age 21 with no money while I fixed up my financial situation was that I had nothing to do – and all the time to study. Proudly when I re-sat my high school exams I scored in the top 10% the second time around.

107 / Coincidentally, the first work suit I ever purchased.

edly that it's okay to use more than a tiny amount of shampoo.

And while these shortcomings are an inevitable result of a lifetime of pushing myself 'up', the good news is I know what I'm saying is legitimate. I didn't write this book because I 'saw a gap in the market' and swooped in to make a few bucks; I wrote this book because I needed it when I was sixteen and felt completely overwhelmed stepping outside of my regular environment for the first time.

And if this book could help a broke kid with no direction, no motivation, and essentially no chance of making it, I didn't want to keep the information to myself.

No matter where you find yourself right now, from broke with no direction to well-off and still not living your ideal lifestyle, the three step framework contained in this book can help you arrange your thoughts and your actions to get the most out of your life.

So do I know everything? Not at all.

And do I walk around like an insufferable ass, telling everyone I'm living 'my ideal lifestyle'? No. I'm on a journey too, one that I never really expect to finalise.

And I'll be honest about another thing too: I don't always stick to my banking plan perfectly. Sometimes I overspend on a busy weekend and need to dip into my Lifestyle Bucket. But guess what: the world doesn't come crashing down. If I can do the right thing ninety percent of the time, because I have my finances on automation, I know the rest will take care of itself.

If someone who grew up with more knowledge of how to apply

for unemployment benefits than university can turn things around with what is in this book, I'd say there is a chance you can too.

This system worked for me and I believe it'll work for you too. I hope it does. But I also hope you show yourself understanding and compassion. Looking back at my hyper-frugal stage, I see that it was bordering on (or way over the border of) self-neglect. Don't do that. You deserve to get what you want in the short term *and* the long term. You can dip into one of your buckets if you need to – it's your life.

To me, that's what funding your ideal lifestyle means: being able to give yourself the things you really want without it impacting on your long term security.

The good news? You're probably closer to living your ideal lifestyle than you think.

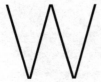e're here. We made it.

Congratulations. You now have some work ahead.

I briefly mentioned this earlier, but as of now, you have the responsibility to yourself to start implementing these ideas. With unlimited access to information, information in itself has become worthless. Worse than worthless, information is now just another distraction.

Implementation on the other hand is valuable. Observable change is something our information-heavy society is willing to pay a premium to obtain. Why? Nothing gets done with the information. The power of change comes in the act of implementation.

To that end, I've created a schedule designed to give you some idea of how long to spend on different parts of this book. Some things can be implemented over the course of an afternoon, some over a month and some over the course of your lifetime.

I've done my absolute best to distil all the information contained in this book down to its easiest implementable function.

As additional help, I've created a video series to accompany these chapter summaries. If you would like a copy, feel free to email me via hello@fundyourideallifestyle.com.au.

SECTION I – CLARIFY LIFESTYLE

CHAPTER 1: YOUR PURPOSE

Time Required: Approximately 30 - 90 days

This chapter is without a doubt the most important chapter in the entire book. It could easily be a whole book in itself. It is the rudder to direct you in life and to give you a way to judge all opportunities.

Feel free to spend your time here. There isn't a rush. It's only by pondering on this subject for long enough that you will be able to move forward confidently. The answer to this question is priceless, and I always love hearing it from someone who has spent the time to figure it out. They're always amazing and heartfelt. Once you reach a point where you feel like your purpose in life is uniquely you, share it with me and with everyone else on social media.

CHAPTER 2: YOUR STRENGTHS

Time Required: 2 minutes to decide, six months to implement.

Your strengths are simply combining your purpose in life with your professional skillset. By doing this you can effectively enact your purpose onto the world. The implementation may take some time though. If you are an employee, manoeuvring yourself within your company will require you to convince others, and if that doesn't work finding a position elsewhere can also take some time. If you're an entrepreneur, pivoting your marketing to better serve a new target market can also take some time. Once you make the change however, you will achieve better results with your higher level of insights.

CHAPTER 3: YOUR MOTIVATION

Time Required: 15 minutes

This powerful exercise only needs to be done once, and has an immediate impact. Identify who you don't want to become, and use it to make sure you end up in the opposite direction.

The power is equal parts wanting to do whatever you can to avoid becoming what you least want to end up becoming, and reducing the barrier to success by letting you off the hook to find 'the perfect career choice'. Nothing you pick will be 'perfect'. Removing that barrier will drastically improve your chances of moving forward. The power is in making the decision and gaining momentum.

CHAPTER 4: THOUGHT FOR TODAY

Time Required: 10 minutes to decide, a lifetime to implement

By spending time considering what is important to you, and what your ideal lifestyle looks like on a weekly basis, you will ensure you actually end up doing these things.

CHAPTER 5: THOUGHT FOR TOMORROW

Time Required: In the background for 30 years

Your ideal lifestyle today is about clarifying what you want out of life. Your ideal lifestyle in the future is about building an asset base as large as possible to pay yourself an income when you no longer work. This will give you more options in retirement, and help you continue to fund your ideal lifestyle in the future also – no matter what you want it to be when you get there. Once you calculate your comfort amount and the size of the asset base you need to work towards, this will give you a target to work towards.

SECTION 2 – AUTOMATE CASHFLOW

CHAPTERS 6 - 10

Time Required: 24 hours[108]

Once you know what your ideal lifestyle looks like today, you can calculate the amounts to be filtered out to the five separate buckets. It should only take you 24 hours to set up the required accounts, set the transfers to work automatically, update your payroll to the new account, and organise your fixed costs to come out of the dedicated account.

---

108 / 24 hours with the help of the FYIL calculator www.fundyourideallifestyle.com. au/calculator and organise all the money filtering via automatic transactions.

By removing yourself as the centre of every single financial decision you make, and outsourcing as much as possible to automation, you free your mind from constant distractions and interruptions. By pursuing cognitive minimalism and avoiding decision fatigue, you give yourself the chance to make better decisions in every other area of your professional and personal life.

SECTION 3 – PURCHASE CAPITAL ASSETS

CHAPTER 11: NEVER LOSE MONEY

Time Required: 15 minutes to read the chapter. Then however long it takes you to change your mind if you are making any of the common investment mistakes.

Building an asset base to provide you with an income when you no longer work requires time and good quality assets. There are many mistakes you can make along the way, and it's easy to be dragged off-course with the endless amount of investment opportunities out there. You don't need to spend your life getting good at investing, and you don't need to do anything overly risky. It requires you to increase your intelligence. In fact, avoiding bad investment decisions is probably the best thing you can do for long-term wealth creation.

CHAPTER 12: WHY DIVERSIFICATION WORKS

Time Required: 15 minutes

Figure out what you want out of your investments. Short term investing under five years is taking on a higher level of risk than long term investing. As such, the shorter term your investment timeline – the safer the investment should be. The longer term your investment timeline – the less conservative your investment can be.

CHAPTER 13: A LETTER TO YOUR FUTURE SELF

Time Required: One week

Once you have an investment plan, which tax structure are you going to use? Are you going to build assets in your name as an individual, which comes with the harshest taxation, or are you going to build assets in the legal 'offshore bank account'? Sure you can't spend the money until you need it later in life, but that is the absolute point of investing.

Figuring out which type of super fund appropriate for you is the hardest part, and while I've given some high level general advice, extra research can't hurt. Once you've decided which type of super fund, and which company to use, choosing an appropriate investment mix in the fund shouldn't take too long. Finding all your super money and combining them together will take around a week. You aren't forced to combine them all however if you prefer the insurances inside each one.

CHAPTER 14: INVESTING OFF THE BEATEN TRACK

Time Required: At least one year

If you consider yourself a risky investor, then I've provided you with a way to manage that additional risk using the Taleb-Dalio portfolio. Needless to say, while I've provided you with a way to pursue this if you so desire, in no way does it promise you success on your options or startup investing. The statistics are against you if you do pursue this, but they are not impossible. If you choose to pursue this path, I would say get stuck into the recommended reading and your own additional research for at least a year before going into the real world to build up your experience.

CHAPTER 15: START SMALL, GET SCREWED

Time Required: At least one year

If you are really up for a risky way to invest, putting not just your money but indeed your career options on the line, then there is the possibility of becoming an entrepreneur. We are already starting to see the birth of a new wave of solo entrepreneurs with the rise of contingency employment, and the decline of full-time employment, and of course with the prospect of technology taking up a higher percentage of jobs over time, this type of thinking may indeed slowly become mandatory. Like risky investing, if you do choose this type of investing there will be a lot to learn, and don't expect to be successful straight away.

....

Personally, I'm a big believer in getting whatever you want out of life. If you want to work an okay job to pay the bills so you can glide through without working too hard or putting in too much effort, that's what you will get. If you want to keep improving yourself to get better results over the course of your lifetime, you'll get that.

This book is the culmination of countless people with whom I've had the privilege of sharing conversations regarding their financial decisions. During this process, I realised what I was doing had far bigger implications. Money choices are life choices, and life choices are money choices. They are inextricably linked like the strands of a double helix. They do not operate in vacuums.

As such, this book was written with much more than just my personal opinion. It is the culmination of what worked and what didn't to give an implementable structure to help you decide what you want out of life and how to go about using your money to achieve it. It takes time so don't rush it, and feel free to keep coming back to this book like an old friend to help you through it all.

ACKNOWLEDGEMENTS

Firstly, a massive thank you to my mum. She raised me up to believe I could be anything I wanted and did everything she could to help get me there. When I asked to start a new sport or hobby, she would scrape together the money and pay the registration fee or buy a new piece of equipment. She even had the decency to not get angry with me when I got bored with it the next week and never went back.

To the 'Nambucca boys' who shared the stage with me. What we lacked in musical talent we made up for with self-belief and sheer workload. Those attributes keep me running to this day.

To the poor people who spent their precious time explaining the most rudimentary business lessons to an overzealous rookie, thank you. Starting with the Clifford family who invested in our band despite me having a horrible haircut and far too many ear piercings. Quincy Neufeld, who introduced me to entrepreneurialism. I remember driving together as he pointed to a reflector on the side of the road and said, 'Someone is really rich because they invented that'. My dad, Pete, and my cousin Brad, who let me chew their ear off at age 22 with my 'amazing ideas' which had zero application in the real world, thanks for being kind.

To Matt Rutter, who on top of being an awesome boss introduced me to the crossover between taxation and financial planning, you gave me the perfect way to make numbers mean something to the average person. And of course, your little axe wielding mate, Ian Lewis, who kicked in with a few tips along the way.

Everyone at Dixon Advisory, for working me harder than I knew possible, I couldn't have asked for a better introduction to the world of high performance. I learned more about superannuation legislation than I care to admit. The two Simon's (Thwaites and Kelly) from Horizons, who taught me how to make all this financial tomfoolery sound more human.

Rachael Browne and Michael Gordon, who took a gamble on an awfully young looking 29-year-old to build a Hillross advisory firm and my start-up buddies Phil and Lisa, who told me to 'go as big as you can' when it finally kicked off.

Peter Ivett, for listening to me complain about not having anything to aspire to now that I filled my desire to start a business, and for pushing me down the rabbit hole to discover my purpose when 'more money' was an insufficient motivator.

Andrew Rockliff, for early morning coffees and helping me find my strength by combining my purpose with what I was best at – cash flow.

The guys at Arrive Wealth for allowing a rookie Principal Adviser set up shop with one of the most well respected practices in Sydney. I became a much better adviser because of it.

My clients who entrusted me with their money and life by taking care of their financial decisions. Your questions, feedback and encouragement helped create the entire three-step framework for this book.

My mates and proof readers Craig Martin, Gregg Owens and Van McCormick, your collective ability to tell me I'm waffling on or drifting off topic has been priceless.

Team Austin who made me look a lot better than I actually am. Ann Maynard, your compliments from the first read truly made me realise maybe this hard work pouring everything I knew into a book was all worth it – thanks for making me legible. And Erin Tyler, you totally came through with the goods on the design inside and out. Thank you!

I couldn't have conceived this type of book without the sharing involved with the extended Financial Advice community, Ray Jaramis, Adrian Patty, Alan Earls, Ben Nash, Jenny Pearce, Chris Bates, Phil Thompson, Andy Marshall, Dan Clark, Theo Angelopoulos, Corey Wastle, Paul Mann, Mark Nagle, Dean Holmes, James Millard, Alisdair Barr, Dr Helen Parker, Connie Mckeage, Peter McCarthy, Ian Dunbar, Naomi Christopher, Julian Plummer, Aleks Vickovich, Lea Schodel, Stuart Bell, Muneesh Wadhwa, Ray Djani, James Sutherland, Jess Brady, Shaun Green, Fraser Jack, Kristen Crawford, Eleanor Dartnall, Shane Hay, Brad Fox and Brenton Tong.

Last but not least, the one person who sat through every LCD tanning moment of me feverishly typing away and sculpting these thoughts into something helpful I could provide the world with. Minun rakas, Veera.

C layton is a lifestyle finance expert specialising in cognitive minimalism – the belief that outsourcing the greatest stresses in life such as money to technology and automation, result in better performance across every other area of life.

Standing at the intersection of lifestyle and money, Clayton has built a reputation in the personal finance space as an innovator through his work with XY Adviser and building a unique financial services company.

Clayton spent ten years of his corporate career in accounting and financial advice. He has now turned his attention to financial education delivered online after identifying a broadening gap between what could be offered through financial planning, and what genuinely helped people succeed in achieving what they wanted out of life.

Growing up in a sleepy coastal town where there was never much money floating around, Clayton thought if money was less complicated, there would have been more to share around. This passion to understand and simplify money led him down the path of personal finance. After working in the personal finance space for a decade, he noticed three consistent problems across all demographics:

1. Not enough time
2. Not finding new experiences
3. Not holding on to enough money

These problems boiled down to one thing: people were worried they were wasting their life.

With the passion to simplify money, and the ability to implement unique service offerings in his own business, Clayton created a service to take on the salary of clients, pay their bills, and ensure there was money to go travelling with each year – while simultaneously building an asset base for later in life. What he didn't expect to find was the less interaction people had with their money, the better they were doing in every other part of their personal and professional lives.

Clients began getting promotions, doing better in their personal lives, winning industry-wide awards, going on more vacations, and still building a larger asset base. In many ways, over the course of twelve months, these clients began living a far more ideal version of their life.

With these results, Clayton directed his research to decision fatigue and the cumulative effect incessant choices can have. This light bulb moment was the catalyst for the *FYIL* book, as Clayton realized through taking away his client's burden of having to think about money, he had stumbled upon not just a better way to manage a regular salary, but to manage modern day life.

**BUY TIME, FIND NEW EXPERIENCES
AND KEEP MORE OF WHAT YOU'VE WORKED FOR.**

YOUR
AL
TYLE

CLAYTON DANIEL